Endorsements

Gary's desire in ministry is to be out of work–to train and develop spiritual leaders in the church who can do the work of the ministry. Paul's final words to the elders in Ephesus were, "Guard yourselves and all the flock of which the Holy Spirit has made you overseers. Be shepherds of the church of God, which he bought with his own blood" (Acts 20:28). He then followed up with his benediction; "Now I commit you to God and to the word of his grace." Feeding on the Word and maintaining an intimate, trusting relationship with God are the keys that Gary emphasizes in this fine book. As my pastor, I have often heard him comment, "That's not a hill worth dying on." There are many projects and programs that could be pushed in the church–some good, most not worth dying for. But the one thing that is lacking is the development of men and women of God who consistently practice core spiritual disciplines. "Character counts."

Mark Anderson, *technical consultant in media ministries with Pamir Productions*

My friend, Gary Taylor, has written <u>Transformed Leadership</u> *to help you and your leadership team grow in your personal devotion to Christ and to corporately serve His body. Gary was an "I'll do anything for a laugh" friend before he came to Christ during the summer prior to our senior year in high school. Now he is an "I'll do anything for my Lord" pastor who has faithfully practiced what he has preached – and written – through his years of ministry. That's the power and grace of God's transformation! In his excellent book he writes of the same transforming power and grace that take place through practicing the all-important spiritual disciplines. So get ready to be transformed by the Spirit as you read about Gary's journey and research. It will be worth the trip!*

Scott M. Bailey, *pastor at Majestic Baptist Church, Pueblo West, Colorado*

It has been a great privilege getting to know Gary Taylor and witnessing his passion for leaders who desire a true transformation in their leadership. His book is a tremendous resource for those of us who continually seek resources that point leaders back to the Word of God for principles of leadership. I think Gary has hit the nail on the head by identifying the importance of a leader's spiritual disciplines in his/her ability to be effective in ministry and leadership development. This book has already challenged me in my own commitment to spiritual disciplines. I'm thankful for Gary's willingness to challenge those of us who are leading others in spiritual formation.

Dr. Peggy Banks, *minister of Spiritual Formation at Northwest Bible Church, Dallas, Texas*

Gary Taylor has hit the nail on the head in his approach to understanding a believer's responsibility in the pro-

cess of growing in Christ. Each of us as believers need to be mentored and taught spiritual disciplines which lead to holiness and a greater depth of relationship with Jesus. Take a trip with Gary and learn through his tutelage how to love and know the Savior in greater depth.

Raymond Dickson, *senior project manager and Cisco certified inter-networking expert, St. Louis, Missouri*

What hath spiritual discipline to do with leadership development? A lot, if you ask Dr. Gary Taylor. In a ministry culture obsessed with business tactics and platform-building, Taylor's book is a blast of fresh air. With a keen mind and a shepherd's heart, Taylor describes the disconnect between spiritual formation and leadership, and then provides concrete, practicable ways for leaders to grow. A crucial message for church leaders.

Drew Dyck, *managing editor of Leadership Journal at Christianity Today, Carol Stream, Illinois*

Gary Taylor understands what it takes for life change! He knows that spiritual disciplines are not ends in and of themselves. They are not technological devices that we employ to move the hand of God or assure results in ministry. Disciplines are like sails on a schooner. They don't force a gale to blow, but they are essential for anyone who wants to catch the wind. The wind is blowing in the church, my friends, and Gary is one pastor who's enjoying the ride. Read his book and profit from his life. Your people will thank you for it.

Dr. Dan Jarrell, *teaching pastor at ChangePoint, Anchorage, Alaska*

CHARACTER. It is everything in the life of the Christian leader. In a day of spiritual immaturity in the church and leaders falling by the wayside, we desperately need resources that will help us develop deep, Christlike character as an essential prerequisite to leadership. Unfortunately, as Dr. Taylor identifies, we have too often accepted giftedness, talent, charisma or education as qualifiers instead of what matters most. This book brings unique insight into how to develop and recognize biblically-defined church leadership by one who is an experienced and perceptive leader himself. We look forward to using this resource at our college in training godly and mature Native leaders.

Dr. Jason Koppen, president of Indian Bible
College, Flagstaff, Arizona

In my interaction with pastors and churches, I frequently encounter leaders who quietly express to me that their personal lives feel shallow, empty and powerless. They confide that their ministry does not seem to be a vibrant expression of the living God. The most humbling and wonderful experience for a spiritual leader is to minister knowing God is working through you, but the most frightening is to feel that you are on your own in ministry without God's good hand of blessing. Gary Taylor understands this. Transformed Leadership is about the spiritual leader's life of holiness and character and the power of God to change lives through the transformed life of the leader. This book is a great reminder for every pastor and church that a commitment to a disciplined walk of intimacy with God leads to changed lives, beginning with the pastor's own life.

Dr. Les Lofquist, executive director at IFCA
International, Grandville, Michigan

Transformed
Leadership

the role of spiritual disciplines
in leadership development

Transformed
Leadership

Gary L. Taylor

Foreword by *Knute Larson*

LUCIDBOOKS

Houston, Texas

To Melody,

I dedicate this book to my loving wife of 30 years.

*As my constant companion you have blessed me
as a true source of encouragement and strength.
Throughout our journey together you have provided
a glimpse of Jesus for me to see Him more clearly.*

*You are the most precious person I know and a true
song to my life.*

Gary

Contents

Acknowledgments

I WANT TO PERSONALLY THANK SOME CHRISTIAN leaders who have taken the time to walk with me in the journey of my life. God has uniquely placed these men at strategic points along my Christian life to build, encourage and motivate me.

These men all share the personal testimony of effective biblical leadership that has been enhanced by core spiritual disciplines that have deepened their lives.

Scott Bailey, who took the time during high school days to share his life, family and personal relationship with Jesus with a young man who was far from God.

Dean Wisehart, who as my first pastor took a genuine interest in me, teaching me the truths of the Scripture and providing me with encouragement to walk as a man of God. I look forward to our reunion in heaven.

Dan Snively, who gave direction and clarity to me during college days as the dean of students by providing leadership opportunities to focus my energies toward the prize.

Jeff Kowatch, who was the best man on my wedding day, friend since our time together in college and someone who provided me with a clear picture of a consistent Christ-like walk.

Knute Larson, who has been a true mentor to me and believed in me from our earliest times together. He provided me with a picture of pastoral ministry that has equipped, motivated and encouraged me.

I would also like to thank **Dianne Pitts** for her technical proofreading, **Jerry James** for his theological proofreading and **Raymond Dickson** and his family for reading and offering helpful comments during the process of writing. Special thanks are reserved for my dear helpmate, **Melody**, for the time-consuming work of editing my thoughts into a readable format.

List of Tables and Charts

Preface:
A Personal Journey

I AM SEATED IN A PLANE ON THE RUNWAY AT PORT-
land International Airport awaiting the beginning of
a long anticipated trip. The captain of the plane has
just announced that he has been given clearance for
takeoff. This is just the first leg of the journey that will
result in sharing important principles about spiritual
leadership development with the students and faculty
of Indian Bible College in Flagstaff, Arizona.

This opportunity for ministry really began in a
community church located in the Willamette Valley
of Oregon some twenty years earlier. While I served
as the pastor of this church, one high school student
in the youth group stood out. Today he is the president of Indian Bible College. It is through his invitation that I find myself flying many miles to share what
God has laid on my heart.

Each of our lives tells a different story of a journey
in faith. This book tells my journey. But more important, it goes much further to tell about the Christian
journey of life and how to begin well in order to finish

strong. Setting the proper foundation of incorporating spiritual disciplines into daily life and allowing the Holy Spirit to teach and guide are necessary for the journey. It is my prayer that this book will be a helpful guide along your path.

Gary Taylor
Scio, Oregon
February 2013

Foreword

MANY OF US KNOW THE STORY ABOUT THE GREAT Green Bay Packers football coach and icon, Vince Lombardi (second only to Knute Rockne as the greatest football coach ever!). At the start of a session to motivate his team that had been clobbered the day before in a Sunday game, he dramatically and quietly held up a football and stated deliberately, "Gentlemen, this is a football."

Back to the basics.

For the pastor and the student and anyone loving the church, that is what this book is. This is the pastor.

Whether or not you have been clobbered by the church, it will be worth the read. It is back to the Scripture and the basics, with a major on character and how it is developed and strengthened.

If you wish one of the how-to books about church leadership and growth, check one of the many good ones. They will vary, and the writers will tell you what worked where they lived.

But read this one first. It will coincide with the call in the Bible, and be good wherever you live.

In Part One, Gary bluntly states the need for personal character over church strategy, notes all the qualifications from the Bible for elders and pastors, and emphasizes the loving heart of the shepherd. If you know him, you know that is who he is. His definition of a calling to this privilege is strong, feasible and very personal. And his look at the Bible's list of character traits for a good leader is a great reminder for all of us. I love the general description of what shepherding looks like in any size church.

There are many duties for a good pastor, but Gary is loving in his determination that the shepherd graces must prevail in the pulpit and the hallways and one-on-one.

Part Two is CSDs and ELMs, Core Spiritual Disciplines and Effective Leadership Marks, and the areas of theology that back them up. I know Gary Taylor well enough to know that he "eats this stuff up," as we used to say in high school. That is, this stuff about character and personal spiritual disciplines. Actually, he swallows it, if I may press the analogy. He makes it his own.

There are many ways to lead a church or a classroom, and a lot of them work, whatever that means to God. Gary leads by character, and we know what that means to God. And this book is his passion for all of us to check our own spiritual strength, and to make character our daily priority – no matter what Christian magazines and schools call success.

Part Three gives an analysis of the survey of pastors and leaders that Gary took, and how the practice of the disciplines relates to the work of the pastor shepherd. Again, the priority is on strengthening our hearts, not our growth strategy.

Foreword

This book is Gary the coach and pastor at his best, and it is also the best of the Word of God about the servant leader. I am delighted to help him hold it up to say to all who are on the team, "This is a pastor."

Knute Larson, pastoral coach
Sawyer, Michigan
Pastor, The Chapel, Akron, Ohio 1983-2009

"Prayer is the mounting up of the soul to God in the act of worship."

John Smith, *Lectures on the Nature and End of the Sacred Office* (Baltimore: A. Neal, 1810), 31.

"We must depend on the strength of the Lord God for assistance, and for the working of all our works in us and for us."

Matthew Henry, *Communicant's Companion* (New York: L. and F. Lockwood, 1819), 101.

Introduction:
God Has a Plan

THE NEED OF THE CHURCH IN AMERICA TODAY IS holiness. We have substituted talent for transformation and skill for sanctification in the church. But church leaders cannot rely on talent and charisma. They must nurture holiness.

When lives are transformed, wholeness and holiness result. Scripture provides the basis for transformation to take place, and addressing this must include spiritual disciplines. Prayer, confession, Bible study and other spiritual disciplines not only begin but deepen one's intimacy with God. They need to be practiced to build every believer's relationship with God and grow into His likeness. When woven into the daily events of life, disciplines have their greatest personal worth. Individuals and church leaders each become more effective in their spiritual lives. The more disciplines are practiced, the more effective leadership marks become apparent among the body of believers. As a result, the church becomes healthier. The whole church benefits when its leaders are transformed.

1

This book intentionally addresses four groups in the church. First, all people attending church will be challenged to practice spiritual disciplines. It will also challenge those who are training for Christian leadership, as well as pulpit committees, to stress that spiritual disciplines need to be found in a Christian leader. Finally, pastors will be challenged to personally incorporate spiritual disciplines into daily life to an even greater degree than before and urge the people they shepherd to do the same.

Spiritual disciplines supply the supportive structure for the transformation of Romans 12:1-2 to take place. "Therefore, I urge you brothers, in view of God's mercy, to offer your bodies as living sacrifices, holy and pleasing to God – which is your spiritual worship. Do not conform any longer to the pattern of this world, but be transformed by the renewing of your mind. Then you will be able to test and approve what God's will is – his good, pleasing and perfect will" (Rom. 12:1-2).

part one

Setting the Course

"…the Scriptures are shallow enough for the babe to come and drink without fear of drowning and deep enough for theologians to swim in without ever touching bottom."

Walter Henrichsen, *Disciples are Made – not born* (Wheaton, IL: Victor, 1974), 13.

"The humblest, weakest believer possesses a knowledge of God, hidden from the wisest of enlightened men."

Archibald Alexander, *Thoughts on Religious Experience* (Philadelphia: Presbyterian Board of Publication, 1844), 86.

"Leadership is not about personality, possessions, or charisma, but all about who you are as a person. I used to believe that leadership was about style but now I know that leadership is about substance, namely character."

James C. Hunter, *Servant* (New York: Crown Business, 1998), 166.

chapter one

The Prerequisite

"HOW CAN THIS BE?" I ASKED MYSELF AS I LIStened to a church leader tell me he'd never been taught the truths of Scripture by anyone. As he went on, I learned that the difficulty was in applying the truths of the Bible to his personal life. He had been in church leadership for over twenty years and did not know how to put truth into practice. My years of ministry have taught me that this situation is not an isolated one.

Church leaders need to be grounded in God's Word and able to apply it to their lives, as well as have a vision for others to do the same. Later in this book, we'll see from studies of real people in real churches that those who are learning and practicing spiritual disciplines have increased ability to become effective leaders. We'll look closely at leaders, including their qualifications, preparations and tasks. We'll go on to explore what spiritual disciplines are, what marks of leadership develop in those who practice them and how to make this information useful to believers and the church-at-large. We'll see the answer to the question, "What do spiritual disciplines have to do with leadership development?"

The connection is not always made between spiritual disciplines and the biblical qualifications of leadership. It is my observation that spiritual disciplines are seen as non-essential or optional in a believer's life. Mature leaders must be chosen from among the body of believers in a church, and those who are chosen must practice spiritual disciplines.

That is why a seasoned pastor earnestly told me from his own experience, "When the church you pastor chooses elders, make sure they are committed to prayer. If they are not, the church is headed for trouble." It is not enough just to choose elders but to choose those who show evidence of practicing spiritual disciplines in their lives. Paul warned Timothy to be very deliberate in the selection of elders by stating, "Do not be hasty in the laying on of hands" (1 Tim. 5:22). Sadly, in many churches when there is a vacancy in an official position, a church leader is chosen just to fill the vacant office rather than an individual who meets biblical qualifications. This kind of action is detrimental to the church. More effective leadership results when spiritual disciplines are purposefully and noticeably incorporated into life and practice.

Before going further, let's define some terms. This book focuses on Christians, those who believe in Jesus Christ and follow His teachings found in the Bible. The Christian church is another focus and refers to all believers in Jesus Christ or a particular group of believers gathered in a specific location.

Spiritual disciplines are practices found in the Bible that connect the believer to God. The connection between the believer and God is essential to Christian growth and maturity. Not all spiritual disciplines found in Scripture will be emphasized here. We'll look at eight as core spiritual disciplines (CSDs) for the purpose of this book. They are confession, fasting, life together, prayer, service, silence, study and worship.

This book is about church leadership, so not all leadership characteristics found in the business world will be emphasized. For our purpose, we'll look at eight effective leadership marks (ELMs) which help those who lead an individual or group and will be studied from the perspective of the life of the apostle Paul. They are enthusiasm, faith, hope, humility, integrity, knowledge, love and vision.

As for the offices of church leadership, we'll target the New Testament offices of elder, pastor and deacon.

Not long ago I received a telephone call from a colleague sharing his frustrations with pastoral search committees. The longer the discussion lasted, the more common topics kept surfacing. Philosophy, programming or doctrinal issues were at the center of nearly every interview question he'd been asked. As he continued the conversation, his voice intensifying, he declared that search committees ask nothing about spiritual disciplines. His conclusion? Pastoral search committees desire skilled pastors rather than sanctified ones and talent rather than transformation.

Author Robert Anderson, in his advice to pastors who are asked to complete references for ministerial candidates, notes that inquiries are made about abilities of the person being considered, his personality traits and the talents of his wife but rarely about character traits.[1] During the last three decades, I have observed seminary students training for church leadership, pastors in active ministry positions and church leaders (deacons and elders) on countless occasions. Conversations with these people have shown me that CSDs tend to be weak areas in their lives and those of other Christian leaders. Unfortunately, this problem is not new. Francois Fenelon, the French archbishop, theologian and poet writing in the seventeenth century, referred to character as a greater prize than health.[2] Writing in the nineteenth century, Charles Bridges referred to true character and substance as being essential qualities to look for in a pastor of a church.[3] Were they lacking in his day, too? Recently, while speaking about these issues with the chairman of the leadership team at the church I currently pastor, he shared that character and being a growing Christian are more important than all the education and training in the world.

During the past few years the church has been regularly assaulted with scandals involving its leaders ranging from financial to sexual. Sexual misconduct by Christian leaders causes great pain to individual lives and damages the testimony of the church. In many cases these leaders had been very effective in their ministry prior to the scandal. They were people of talent, charisma, ability and charm. Afterward they want to hide their sinful actions for fear of becoming found out and exposed. Fenelon referred to these people as being "full of themselves too much to hear God. These turn everything to reasoning. They seek in natural wisdom, and in prudence, what would come to us infinitely better through the simplicity and the quietness of the Spirit of God."⁴ But Paul told Timothy, "The sins of some men are obvious, reaching the place of judgment ahead of them; the sins of others trail behind them" (1 Tim. 5:24).

Scandals within the church including sexual misconduct and financial indiscretion can be traced back to spiritual weakness in the leaders who fell to temptation. Can it be that they fell to a particular temptation because Satan found and attacked the weakest area in their spiritual armor?

Temptation in an individual's life is harder to resist when one is weak spiritually. Weakness can occur as a result of not practicing CSDs. In this way, one becomes weak and allows for temptation to have further inroads into his or her life. Jesus described this situation by stating, "...in the time of testing they fall away" (Luke 8:13). When spiritual defenses are lowered, the enemy gains a foothold from which to attack believers. Men and women do not possess the capacity to overcome sin and evil on their own. The Psalmist declared, "How can a young man keep his way pure? By living according to your word. I seek you with all of my heart; do not let me stray from your commands. I have hidden your word in my heart that I might not sin against you" (Ps. 119:9-11).

Warfare in the spiritual realm is real; everyone must recognize this and prepare for it. Paul warned the Ephesian church when he penned these words, "For our struggle is not against flesh and blood, but against the powers of this dark world and against the spiritual forces of evil in the heavenly realms" (Ephesians 6:12). Gordon MacDonald points out, "Study the tragic moments in many lives, and you will often discover that a secondary set of conditions was right behind the reality of embedded evil. These conditions weakened the resolve of a man or woman to resist temptation and make decisions that were not right or true."[5]

MacDonald claims, "The word scandal is often employed for such occasions of optimum failure. It suggests the revelation of an act or action entirely opposite our convictions and expectations. Because of the nature of human beings, we will always have scandals with us, and – sorry to say – it is always possible that we will be the scandal."[6]

These are sobering words indeed! The church needs to wake up to the warning signs and separate itself from the evil waiting for it. The truth is, we are all fallen people, whether or not we are guilty of misbehavior.[7] The church and especially its leaders must be prepared to prevent scandals from taking place in Christian lives. Peter warned, "Be self-controlled and alert. Your enemy the devil prowls around like a roaring lion looking for someone to devour" (1 Pet. 5:8).

In recent years the church has been helped by a number of authors who have written books on the subjects of the church, leadership and being a pastor. In reading these books, I have been both blessed and discouraged. My observation is that current literature on these topics lacks good strategy for using spiritual disciplines in the development of leadership for the church. (For a more thorough treatment of specific books and their authors, see my doctoral dissertation.[8]) This shows the need for a fresh, renewed look at the role of spiritual disciplines as the key to effective leadership development in the church-at-large. My present ministry as pastor and educator also shows the timeliness of this topic.

Desiring to help leaders grow in their personal commitment to Christ and understand the role of spiritual disciplines in their lives has been a driving force in my ministry. As shepherd of a flock, I find it my responsibility and privilege to guide the church and its leaders along paths of growth and practice. Developing spiritual leadership is a special concern to me as a pastor because it is what gives the church its present and future ministry.

About leadership training, J. Oswald Sanders correctly asserted that it "cannot be done by employing the techniques of mass production. …[Leaders] are produced one by one, because someone has taken the pains to discipline, to instruct and enlighten, to nurture and train the one that is younger."[9] Building leaders takes time. This process cannot be done by listening to a series of lectures or reading a good book. Do not allow your strengths about leadership training to be shaped by our culture of mass production and quick results. God will shape each leader into a useful vessel in His time through life experiences, training, suffering and discipline (Heb. 12:11).

Is it true that the Bible's emphasis is on people, not methods? That the crucial factor in God's work is the leader? Throughout Scripture, God is looking for and then laying His hand on some man or woman to accomplish His will.

This is not said to minimize the value of methods. We must not be slothful in business and only fervent in spirit serving the Lord. We must do both. Our instruction from Paul is to do things decently and in order (1 Cor. 14:40). Scripture is clear in the matter of God seeking (John 4:23), calling (2 Tim. 1:9), sending (Isa. 6:8), equipping (Eph. 4:12) and blessing (Rom. 15:29) people, not methods. The leader is crucial; methods are complementary. The leader is primary; techniques are secondary.

In another chapter we'll present the characteristics that made a particular leader stand apart, a great and inspiring leader whose influence and inspiration have meant so much to the Christian church. There is hardly a leader whose influence has been quite as profound as the apostle Paul.

What made him this kind of leader? As with every other person worthy of the title, it was not necessarily because he chose or was determined to be. As we look at the man himself, we see that it was his personal characteristics that placed him in this position of leadership. The ELMs previously listed come from Paul's life as they are described in Scripture.

It has been my observation while in Christian ministry that spiritual disciplines are rarely mentioned in what is required of the leader and the development of that leader. Yet it can be shown that there are correlations between spiritual disciplines and marks of leadership. For instance, what is the connection between studying God's Word and having vision for the church? Does the discipline of fasting affect one's faith? What makes the leadership in urban settings so different from the rural? In what ways and settings do CSDs influence matters of integrity in a leader's life?

The research that helped answer the above questions was conducted in a number of churches varying in size, demographics, denomination and location. The resulting principles will apply to all churches. Leadership development within the local church has no size or demographic constraints. Neither is the location or denomination of a particular church a central factor in leadership development. All churches can and should strive to develop leadership from within. However, not all churches are healthy. In those cases where the church is lacking biblically qualified leadership, it should approach local healthier churches for assistance. Qualified leaders from healthier churches might come to the church that is asking for help to train others over a period of time. Or the church asking for help might send potential leaders to the healthier church to be mentored by capable men. Either type of exchange can provide the help that is needed to ultimately build healthy leadership from within a church. When it comes to training biblically qualified leaders within the local church, we must resist the temptation of hastily selecting leaders (many, perhaps, not biblically qualified). I believe churches would be much stronger and healthier by choosing to train leaders before they enter the sphere of church leadership rather than after they are selected for the leadership position.

Fruitful spiritual leadership within the local church begins at its foundational base with an individual's salvation experience when they make a personal commitment to the Lord (John 3:16). As each believer grows in his or her relationship with the Lord, some type of personal growth strategy is developed (2 Tim. 2:15). Each strategy will look different since the way growth occurs varies from person to person.

This conscious effort to grow can include a time set aside for prayer and Bible study, a short-term mission trip or an accountability group. With growth comes concern for others (Rom. 12:5), since the focus next moves outward in service and ministry. Finally, spiritual leadership emerges when the mature believer is able to practice and teach others the truths of Scripture (2 Tim. 2:2). The following diagram shows how spiritual leadership is developed.

Personal
Committment
to Christ

Strategy for Personal Growth

Concern for Others

Able to Teach

Fruitful Spiritual Leadership

Spiritual disciplines have much to do with leadership development in the church. As M. Robert Mulholland shares, the only pure motive of our spiritual disciplines is the motive of our loving obedience to God.[10] The first step of obedience is making a personal commitment to Christ. This begins with prayer, the simplest of disciplines. Then as the believer grows in love with God and practices more spiritual disciplines out of obedience to Him, he or she will move through successive levels: establishing a strategy for personal growth which spreads to a concern for spiritual growth in others which works its way out through teaching others the truths of Scripture. As loving obedience for God grows, so does our fruitful spiritual leadership toward others. These two principles go hand in hand, and well they should. We must never accept short-term success for long-term effectiveness in the local church.

Spiritual disciplines are so vital to the process that without them, the character qualities of First Timothy 3:1-7 and Titus 1:6-9 may never be fully embraced in a leader's life. These are, in fact, the qualifications for elders and deacons.

Leaders who are performance-driven have a powerful urge to direct spiritual disciplines into works of righteousness.[11] These wrong motives can lead to legalism in the Christian life and are very dangerous to believers. A clear distinction needs to be made: spiritual disciplines being practiced do not make a good leader, they enhance it. Only God raises up His servant leaders. It is by His power and His blessing. God's grace upon the life of an individual is not bought or stolen; it is a gift from the Father (Eph. 2:8-9). With this distinction in our minds, we can see that the role of spiritual disciplines under the proper guidance of God is crucial to leadership development in the local church.

Some specific benefits of teaching and practicing spiritual disciplines include greater pastoral staff unity of purpose and effectiveness. Also, seminary students who exercise spiritual disciplines will gain an excellent training resource for personal holiness. Lay leadership in the local church will benefit in the areas of personal holiness and leadership training. The principles shared in the chapters to follow will give pastors new insights for guiding the spiritual development of men and women in their churches. Our fruitful spiritual leadership in loving obedience to God is the primary task before us.

chapter two

The Mandate

PERHAPS YOU'VE SEEN "WAY TO EMMAUS," A classic painting done in 1877 by Robert Zund. Three men are talking earnestly as they walk together along a path shaded by tall trees. Let that image come to life in your mind for a few moments, for it gives helpful insights about building church leaders today (Luke 24:13-35).

The men walk beside one another along the road. This shows the close proximity, intimacy and perhaps urgency, we must have with one another through the process of instruction in the Christian life (2 Tim. 2:2).

The men appear purposeful and headed toward a goal. The setting of the painting is on the road to Emmaus soon after Jesus's crucifixion when two of these men are full of questions about what had happened to their Lord and the meaning of it all. What they wanted to know was more about the Savior. Jesus, the third man, came along beside them, unknown to them at the time, and provides the knowledge they seek. When we provide knowledge of the Savior to others, we are really building leaders for the future (Acts 3:14-47).

The road is like other roads, straight in some places and curved in others, as it continues toward its destination. Those who build leaders find similar variations along their route. Sometimes progress is steady, others times slowed; but growing in the knowledge of our Savior ultimately needs to go on despite inevitable delays. Even Jesus knew of the urgency and difficulty men would have in following Him when He asked the disciples, "You do not want to leave too, do you?" (John 6:67). Building leaders stands or falls with two words, "faithful men." Faithful men and women have always been in short supply, but they must be sought to build leaders (Prov. 20:6). A life spent building leaders for the kingdom is never easy. Take courage, though, for the road to building leaders has been designed by God with our best interests at heart.

The road is uneven in spots with unexpected dips and holes. In similar ways, obstacles, whether physical or spiritual, may come without warning along the way of building leaders. Looking ahead and planning accordingly are essential. While living in Indiana during my college days, I often passed by the concrete foundation of an unfinished hospital. The building gave every appearance of a promising structure by the massive foundation. The foundation remained in its unfinished form for several years and then was demolished. The sight of that unfinished building stood as a monument to poor planning. Similarly, when building leaders, our willful planning is involved in the process. Poor planning by the participants and not counting the cost lead to abandonment of the plan.

The men look intently at Jesus. We need to keep our attention focused on Christ to stay on course and not get side tracked. Just before I began seminary, I worked as a farmhand on a large dairy operation in Ohio. I was asked one day to take the tractor into the field to prepare the ground for planting. The experienced farmer must have known something was wrong by my puzzled expression and asked if I had any questions. I told him I didn't know how to keep the rows straight in the field. The answer came back to me with a warm smile and nod toward the field, "See the fence posts at the other end? Keep your eyes on only one post and head the tractor straight for it." This illustration has served me well over the years while encouraging men and women to keep their attention focused on Christ in order to stay on course (Heb. 12:1-2).

Jesus is with them. He was dead and now lives forever and ever (Rev. 1:8). He walks with us in our experiences and speaks to us through His Word. He promised never to leave us alone (Matt. 28:20).

The scriptural mandate, comprised of making disciples (Matt. 28:19-20) and committing the truth of the gospel to other men (2 Tim. 2:2), is established in the Bible. Let's go on to describe this mandate of instruction by looking at the early church, leaders in the church today and the timeless shepherding model presented in Scripture.

THE EARLY CHURCH

The book of Acts provides Christians with information about the early church that is both foundational and insightful. It's author, Luke, wrote about how the church began, what the basic leadership was, existing tensions among believers and how the gospel spread in that day.

The foundation of the church is Jesus Christ. "For no one can lay any foundation other than the one already laid, which is Christ Jesus" (1 Cor. 3:11). He chose disciples to occupy a place in that foundation with Him (Eph. 2:20). Jesus is also the cornerstone of that foundation by virtue of His death and resurrection. "He is 'the stone you builders rejected, which has become the capstone'" (Acts 4:11). The church was also purchased with His own blood according to Luke: "Keep watch over yourselves and all the flock of which the Holy Spirit has made you overseers. Be shepherds of the church of God, which He bought with his own blood" (Acts 20:28). Jesus is the Head over the church (Eph. 1:20-23), and He gives gifts to members of His body (Eph. 4:8). The church was activated and energized by the Holy Spirit whom Jesus sent (Acts 2:33). Christ is the founder of the church and chose the apostles to be part of that foundation. He gave basic teaching concerning relationships in the church and gave His life to become the cornerstone. On the day of Pentecost, He sent the Holy Spirit to activate the church. An immediate effect was produced upon the people gathered at Pentecost who heard Peter preach (Acts 2:37).

The products of Pentecost to the church are recorded with great clarity in Acts 2:42-47. The early believers "devoted themselves ..." (Acts 2:42). To be devoted is to have a single-minded fidelity to a certain direction or action. Together and faithfully, they held on to the apostles' teaching, fellowship, the breaking of bread and prayer. The results of such devotion included awe among the believers, favor with all men and new converts added daily.

The early believers "devoted themselves to the apostles' teaching...." This indicates that there were already in the church some settled forms of teaching that eventually developed into creeds. The apostles' teaching included basic theological principles and the essential truths of the gospel. Believers established a pattern of steadfast and single-minded devotion to hearing what the apostles had to say. "Let the word of Christ dwell in you richly as you teach and admonish one another with all wisdom, and as you sing songs, hymns and spiritual songs with gratitude in your hearts to God" (Col. 3:16). This means for us today that until our teaching is right, our lives will be wrong.

The believers of the early church "devoted themselves to ... fellowship" (Acts 2:42). Here we see the first mention of *koinonia* in the New Testament. The word *koinonia* conveys the idea of believers holding things in common. Fellowship is sharing a common religious experience, goods and a common meal together. The emphasis of the Acts 2 passage is on contributing and giving toward the needs of others. In the early church, fellowship rested on mutual generosity and sharing in the needs of others. They belonged to one another. Today, believers should hunger for such togetherness and love. We must continue to gather together under the royal banner stained by the blood of Christ. The church should be a great movement marching shoulder to shoulder under the name of Jesus. However, this biblical concept has fallen on hard times in our modern age, for when we say the word *koinonia*, the image of cookies and punch comes to mind. How sad, because *koinonia* literally cost something to the early church (2 Cor. 8:4; 9:13; 13:14; Acts 2:44-45). Fellowship is also seen as a work of the Spirit (1 John 1:3) and takes place when we draw near to God (2 Cor. 8:4). So the next time someone says, "Come on over, and let's have fellowship," pause and ask yourself what Jesus and the early believers might think of that.

The believers "devoted themselves to the breaking of bread and ...prayer" (Acts 2:42). Christ's atonement was constantly before them by the breaking of bread together, and the hearts of the believers moved upward through prayer. Prayer is our personal communication with God: our requests, praise and intercession. There is great advantage to common prayer and common praise. This is worship.

Luke records in Acts 2:43 that everyone was filled with awe. Signs and wonders were being done by the apostles. Belongings were shared in common and needs were being met (Acts 2:44).

This image of the church is a radical reorientation of essential relationships (Acts 2:46). The early Christians ate meals together with gladness and sincerity of hearts. When people outside of the fellowship of the church saw how Christians behaved toward one another, they were drawn to this incredible love. It was no wonder that the early church also received new converts daily (Acts 2:47). There evidently was continuous revival day by day. Evangelism was the natural course of these events and recorded as a response to Peter's sermon.

LEADERS IN THE CHURCH TODAY

The image you may have in your mind of a church leader (pastor, elder or deacon) may differ significantly from the image another person has. In fact, the image one has of the Christian ministry may be confusing. To some, the image of a pastor or church leader is something like a religious knight in shining armor who does battle with the evil forces of darkness as he goes about calling on parishioners. This mythical pastor is always winning battles and placing another notch on his spiritual belt after each victory. He immediately knows the right answers to the theological questions posed to him. This man is heaven-sent, and it is difficult for people at church to see him any other way. Although this image is a bit overstated, it is real in the minds of a certain number of people who attend church.

For others, however, the image of a pastor is negative. It is the image of a hypocritical and morally bankrupt individual, one who fleeces the sheep and thinks nothing of it. A pastor can do no good in the eyes of this group of people.

Another image of the pastor shifts back and forth between the two described above. Those who hold this view have difficulty understanding the duties and ministry of a pastor because they've seen church leaders lovingly lead people through times of tragedy and loss. Yet on other occasions, church leaders and pastors appear to them to be hopelessly outdated and out of touch. These people view the pastor as neither good nor bad but rather neutral.

A story is told of a church that was having a difficult time securing the right candidate in their pastoral search. Candidate after candidate had been interviewed and rejected because of small imperfections. Finally one of the board members asked to share a letter. Standing, he read: "Gentleman, understanding your pulpit is vacant, I would like to apply for the position. I have many qualifications. I have been a preacher with much success and also had some success as a writer. Some say I am a good organizer. I have been a leader most places I have been. I am over fifty years of age. I have never preached in one place more than three years. In some places I have left town after my work has caused riots and disturbances. I must admit I have been in jail three or four times, but not because of any real wrongdoing. My health is not too good, although I still get a great deal done. The churches I have preached in have been small, although located in several large cities. I've not gotten along well with religious leaders in the towns where I've preached. In fact, some have threatened me and even attacked me physically. I am not too good at keeping records. I have been known to forget whom I have baptized. However, if you can use me, I shall do my best for you."

You can imagine how the congregation reacted when this letter was read. The members were indignant. How could they select a pastoral leader who is aged, sick and a guest of prisons? They asked the board member why he had wasted their time with this letter. The board member replied, "It is signed, the Apostle Paul."

Real or not, these images of the pastor are out of focus. Where can we turn for answers? There is only one handbook that describes the pastoral role sufficiently. The Bible is the only source of authoritative information to help the church of Christ in this matter. The Bible provides the right model, characteristics and tasks for the man who sets his heart on being a pastor.

Today's churches need to focus on the message Paul provides for effective Christian service as it relates to leadership qualities. Surely, the life and words of Paul offer us mature advice on these subjects.

Paul gave pastoral counsel to Timothy in the book of Second Timothy. The pastor is to preach the Word of God (4:2). He is to watch over the people entrusted to his care (4:5). He is to do the work of ministry to the glory of God and on behalf of a congregation of saints (2:24-26). These three roles have helped inform the church's understanding of pastoral theology down through the centuries.

What Paul provides as advice to pastors is not necessarily confined to them. Lay ministers, paid ministers and member ministers (laymen) alike need to take this message seriously. Unless all Christians heed Paul's advice, the great tasks of "making disciples" and sharing the good news will remain unfinished.

The ministry that Paul describes must occur for the church of any size to be healthy. It is my observation that the trend of medium (200-500 people) and large (500 plus people) churches today is for the pastor to specialize in ministry settings, while in the small church (up to 200 people), the pastor is a generalist. Specializing in ministry might describe pastors who are specifically trained in a particular skill used in ministry settings (youth, children's, pastoral care, mission, or Christian education to name a few). Being a generalist in the ministry setting means that the pastor is in charge of completing or equipping others to do the general work of ministry that is needed in every church. Because of ever increasing financial matters facing the church, there is a rethinking of this strategy. Many medium- and larger-sized churches are being forced to cut staff positions to save money. These financial constraints are causing churches of all sizes to revisit the "generalist" model of shepherding. When pastoral leadership specializes, important functions once done by the pastor are left undone. To balance the demands of ministry, lay leadership is often utilized to discharge certain duties of ministry. But lay leadership must be trained adequately in the duties of spiritual care. Ephesians 4:11-16 provides clear instruction to the pastor for equipping the saints to do these works of ministry. A balance at this time in the life of the church would enhance the classical care of ministry laid out before us by Paul in Ephesians. This understanding would also utilize large numbers of lay ministers within the church.

Some would say that the church of today is in crisis. Training institutions for pastors appear to have declining interest and enrollment. Some report that increasing numbers of pastors are leaving their calling and resigning from their shepherding roles to find secular employment. I submit that although these reports may be true, the best days of the church are still ahead. God is still on the throne. He still cares for and loves the church for whom He died. These challenges facing churches and pastors today are opportunities! Pastors must pray, seek out and train member ministers to do some of the tasks of ministry. Pastors and lay leaders need to partner together. We need to seek the same opportunities for balance that confronted the early church in Acts 6:1-7. The Bible exhorts the pastor to serve the church in this way. Jesus promised that the gates of Hell would not succeed in overcoming the church (Matt. 16:18).

The member minister who aspires to leadership and pastors in the local church can find their charted course in the Bible. Leadership in the local church needs to have a Christ-centered image of the church. With Jesus Christ at the center of church ministry, Satan cannot possibly win.

SHEPHERDING MODEL

The image of the shepherd in the Bible is clear and undeniable. This imagery of shepherd and flock is consistent throughout the Psalms. You can simply open a concordance and trace the words "shepherd," "flock" and "sheep" through the Psalter. You will discover how God ministers to you and how God expects shepherds to minister. Psalm 23 masterfully uses the descriptive metaphor of shepherding. Tending sheep means that the shepherd will be among them, assisting them, caring for them and defending them. This imagery also appears in Jesus's teaching (Matt. 9:35-38; John 10).

It has been my life long desire to remain fit for pastoral ministry. My strengths and those of my fellow pastor shepherds should be measured in our personal character, calling, and how we perform biblical tasks with the Bible as our standard. Accordingly, let's turn our attention in this section to the biblical qualifications found in the New Testament.

In the books of First Timothy and Titus, the apostle Paul pointed out specific qualifications for those desiring to be elders and deacons in the local church. Qualities of a life are emphasized as opposed to skills, abilities or even spiritual gifts. Concerning these qualities of life Fenelon shared, "Outer works are the fruits and inseparable consequences by which we recognize true devotion. But true devotion, the source of these works, is all in the depths of the heart."[1]

For the purpose of this book, we will concentrate on the lists of qualities that Paul laid down in First Timothy and Titus. Paul emphasized motives, moral and ethical behavior, attitudes, goals and a good reputation. I believe that the emphasis on character is far more important than choosing people with an impressive skill set or vast knowledge. People with exceptional gifts can subtly lead others in the wrong direction with great speed. Such men have tendencies to be very prideful. What Paul is emphasizing are the good character and qualities that help build a good reputation in the church and the community.

The potential of the local church rests primarily in its leaders. We all appreciate direction and leadership but maybe not like the type shown in the following story. A pilot announced over his intercom system, "Ladies and gentlemen, I have good news and bad news. The good news is that we have a tailwind, and we are making excellent time. The bad news is that our compass is broken, and we have no idea where we are going."

Our churches depend on the direction of their leadership. The people of the body will grow no higher than they are challenged to grow by the example of the leadership. Excellent leadership casts vision for the church, identifies needs and deploys the saints to do the work of service. Leaders must be examples of First Thessalonians 4, leading quiet lives, not as "over doers," but as "loving overseers."

Character

The character of a shepherd matters to God, and it should matter to all of us. If one is not a man of character, then he is not much at all. (For a thorough treatment of the character qualifications, see Lea and Griffin's commentary on the books of Timothy and Titus.[2]) The reader should compare First Timothy 3:1-7 with the list in Titus 1:6-9. This list can be viewed in the chart entitled "Biblical Qualifications for Elder" at the end of the First Timothy section of this chapter. For the purpose of this book we will examine the passages of First Timothy 3:1-7, Titus 1:6-9 and First Peter 5:1-4 in order to describe each biblical character trait of the pastor shepherd.

1 Timothy 3:1-7

The overseer must first be "above reproach" (1 Tim. 3:2). There is no hidden agenda or skeletons in the closet that should come out to haunt him. This individual is one who can stand the test of scrutiny because no evil can be found against him. The shepherd should desire to live among the sheep and to live his life as an honorable man. No man living is sinless, but all men must strive to be above reproach. The life of the shepherd must be a demonstration of Christianity for all to see. The single Greek word used for this first quality describes a position that is not open to attack. The shepherd must be of such fine character as to be beyond condemnation. His life should not legitimize or merit any negative condemnation that could be harmful to a Christian leader's testimony.

The Bible calls for the shepherd to be the "husband of one wife" (1 Timothy 3:2). The shepherd should believe in the sanctity of marriage and model this before the sheep. A shepherd must consider marriage to be one of the most valuable assets he has and put much effort toward keeping it alive and well. It is clear that a man's ability to manage his own marriage and home indicates ability to shepherd a flock. Satan is resolute in his desire to destroy the harmony and sanctity of the marriage bond between husband and wife. The interpretation of this small phrase has been disputed by many biblical scholars. (For a fuller treatment of the five different views connected with this qualification, consult the very readable and reliable instruction by New Testament scholar Homer Kent, Jr.[3]) The bottom line for me is that all marital sin should be avoided at all cost and the pastor shepherd must be a "one woman man." There is room for a difference of opinion on this subject, but the "husband of one wife" is the standard set by God. The emphasis is on the character of the pastor shepherd which is at the heart of all biblical character traits.

The shepherd should seek to establish a moderate lifestyle, one that is "temperate" (1 Tim. 3:2) for himself and his family. A shepherd needs to have sensible judgment in all things. Watching over the sheep requires attention and care on the part of the shepherd. Keeping alert and attending to the work of the church is the shepherd's charge.

He should have the desire to be strong and "self-controlled" (1 Tim. 3:2) in behavior and appetites as an example to the flock of God. Having a sound mind with good understanding displays control over one's passions. To be self-controlled is to seek with the Spirit's guidance to control oneself. The shepherd should not exhibit or participate in foolish behavior that could block the gospel message from going forward. Self-control should mark the shepherd's life and thus help him succeed in any task God has in mind for him to do.

The shepherd should do his best to think before speaking and be careful of how he dresses and acts, so as to be "respectable" (1 Tim. 3:2) to those around him and represent Christ well. The church is no place for a shepherd to act as the town jester or clown. A pastor's bearing, appearance, speech and actions should express dignity.

Being "hospitable" (1 Tim. 3:2) does not mean

that the shepherd and spouse have no privacy. It does mean that their home is a tool for ministry to others. Being hospitable conveys the idea of loving the one who is a stranger. This kind of ministry will establish an appropriate model for ministry to the flock. Hospitality was necessary in the early church as there was need for the traveler to rest during a journey.

The shepherd should be "able to teach" (1 Tim. 3:2). A shepherd is automatically a teacher and therefore must be a careful student of the Word of God and able to communicate wisdom to others. One might think that this particular calling is all about teaching or preaching, but I believe that this particular quality is mostly about being a proper model, the most powerful teaching tool of all.

It should be a purpose in the shepherd's life to be "not given to much wine" (1 Tim. 3:3). I believe that addictions of any kind should be personally avoided to present a wholesome and exemplary image for our Lord. The shepherd must seek the assistance of the Holy Spirit in not allowing anything to have mastery over him.

A shepherd is a man who is "not violent" (1 Tim. 3:3). He must not be argumentative or strike a person physically. But he should be a man with backbone who can stand up for what is right. If a shepherd engages in a fight, he should make sure he is fighting Satan and not some other Christian.

The shepherd should strive to be "gentle" (1 Tim. 3:3) and understand that sheep can be injured if he pushes carelessly through obstacles as changes are made within the church or organization. The absence of gentleness in a shepherd's life creates a vacuum that will not be filled by the love of God.

A shepherd should not glory in a good argument and should not be "quarrelsome" (1 Tim. 3:3). Short tempers do not make for long ministries for the shepherd who is disagreeable. Arguments are very destructive in any situation. Rather, the shepherd should be peaceable in conduct and not desire to have the final word in every conversation. Quarrelsome speech keeps one from hearing the voice of God.

The shepherd should be "not a lover of money" (1 Tim. 3:3). God is faithful in meeting the needs of any shepherd and those of his family. A shepherd should be a man of conscience and integrity. Bad stewardship and ethics related to money hinder a shepherd's ministry. The reputation of the elder is at stake with regard to coveting and will cripple the shepherd's ministry.

The shepherd should set a high priority on "managing his own family well" (1 Tim. 3:4). This is not a job that is done alone. The biblical statement presupposes an understanding relationship between the father and his children. The shepherd should be consistent in discipline and true to his words. Commonplace severity and sternness in a shepherd's life will never win the hearts of the family unit. The shepherd who is a father should strive to govern his own house in love.

Excessive force and brutality in no way compliment the father to "see that his children obey him" (1 Tim. 3:4). Rather, the shepherd/elder who finds himself a father must love his children, drawing out of them a natural respect. To the elder (1 Tim. 3:4), the Greek word used for children conveyed the idea of proper respect. To the deacon (1 Tim. 3:8), the Greek work for children conveyed the idea of being worthy of respect. In these two instances the elder is set apart from the deacon and can be seen by the way the Greek words were used and translated. As for the deacon, he is on the level all men should aspire toward.

Shepherds should "not be a recent convert" (1 Tim. 3:6) or newly converted to the Christian faith. The shepherd should be a seasoned man with experience who is renewed by the Lord's mercies day by day. The shepherd should not be "one newly planted" in the Christian faith. It makes sense that someone new to the faith and lacking experience in the ways of God cannot guide the church effectively.

Enjoying a "good reputation with outsiders" is very important for the shepherd (1 Tim. 3:7). Scandals and men go hand in hand. Albert Mohler shares, "Character is indispensable to credibility, and credibility is essential to leadership. The great warning to every leader is that certain sins and scandals can spell the end to our leadership. We can forfeit our role as leader and the stewardship of leadership can be taken from us."[4]

This good reputation conveys the idea of respect from even the outside world of nonbelievers. A shepherd should have good business dealings and a good testimony with the unsaved, be a good neighbor and pay debts promptly.

Biblical Qualifications for Elder		
English Word/ Phrase	**Greek Word/ Phrase**	**Reference**
"above reproach"	*anepilempton*	1 Tim. 3:2
"husband of but one wife"	*mias gunaikos andra*	1 Tim.3:2; Titus 1:6
"temperate"	*nephalion*	1 Tim. 3:2
"self-controlled"; "sensible"	*sophrona*	1 Tim.3:2; Titus 1:8
"respectable"	*kosmion*	1 Tim. 3:2
"hospitable"	*philoxenon*	1 Tim.3:2; Titus 1:8
"able to teach"	*didaktikon*	1 Tim. 3:2
"not given to much wine"	*me paroinon*	1 Tim. 3:3; Titus 1:7
"not violent"	*me plekten*	1 Tim. 3:3; Titus 1:7
"gentle"	*epieike*	1 Tim. 3:3
"not quarrelsome"	*me amachon*	1 Tim. 3:3
"not a lover of money"	*me aphilargyron*	1 Tim. 3:3
"manage own family well"	*idiou oikoukalos proistamenon*	1 Tim. 3:4
"sees that his children obey him"	*tekna exonta en hupotage*	1 Tim. 3:4

"respect"	*semnotetos*	1 Tim. 3:4
"not be a recent convert"	*me neophyton*	1 Tim. 3:6
"a good reputation with outsiders"	*mapturian kalen exein apo ton exothen*	1 Tim. 3:7
"blameless"	*anegkleton*	Titus 1:6-7
"children believe and are not open to the charge of being wild and disobedient"	*tekna echon pista me en kategophia asotias e anupotakta*	Titus 1:6
"not overbearing"	*me authades*	Titus 1:7
"not quick tempered"	*me ophgilon*	Titus 1:7
"not pursuing dishonest gain"	*me aisxrokerde*	Titus 1:7
"loves what is good"	*philagathon*	Titus 1:8
"self-controlled"	*sophrona*	Titus 1:8
"upright"	*dikaion*	Titus 1:8
"holy"	*hosion*	Titus 1:8
"disciplined"	*enkrate*	Titus 1:8
"hold firmly to the trustworthy messages as it has been taught"	*antexomenon tou kata ten didaxen pistou logou*	Titus 1:9

The Mandate

<u>Titus 1:6-9</u>

Paul charged Titus to "appoint elders in every town" (Titus 1:5). Although there are two lists for the qualifications for elders (1 Tim. 3:1-7 and Titus 1:6-9), the lists are not identical. One of the most obvious differences between the two lists is the absence of any deacon qualifications following the Titus passage. This could indicate that the churches Timothy served were more established and that the ones Titus served were newer churches. The more established churches perhaps were developed enough for the need of deacons while the reverse was true in the cases of the new churches. Both passages, however, insist on the character of the elder to be blameless. Character counts.

The elder must strive to be "blameless" (Titus 1:6) in the domestic area of his life. To be blameless is to be above reproach. Although two different Greek words were used in First Timothy 3:2 and Titus 1:7 to describe this characteristic, they both convey the same general idea. The domestic area reveals two crucial components. The first is to be the "husband of but one wife" (Titus 1:6). Marital faithfulness was very crucial to Paul's selection process of the elder and should be just as crucial to the church today. The second domestic area has to do with children. Titus 1:6 recorded that "children believe and are not open to the charge of being wild and disobedient." Paul's instructions to Titus conveyed the idea of the elder's children sharing his Christian faith and not living in a manner of wild disobedience while under the authority of the elder.

Introducing the list of qualities found in verses seven and eight, Paul used "blameless" again as in verse six. Five negative characteristics emerge in succession. The first is "not overbearing" (Titus 1:7) or having a desire to only seek pleasure for himself. This pleasure-seeking man who disregards others has no place in pastoral work. Secondly, the elder is "not quick-tempered" (Titus 1:7). The image of a lighted fuse on the end of a stick of dynamite comes to mind when considering this person. For this individual, anger can easily flare up because his temper is not under control. Third, we see that the elder is "not given to much wine" (Titus 1:7). See the comments of this characteristic in the preceding section on First Timothy. Wine is not prohibited here, but dependence is. Fourth, we note that the elder must be "not violent" (Titus 1:7). See the previous notes on First Timothy as the same phrase is used. Lastly, we see that the shepherd is "not pursuing dishonest gain" (Titus 1:7). The making of money is not prohibited here but rather the abuse of it. The shepherd of the flock should not use the high office of leadership in the church to pursue money in dishonest ways.

Paul presented next the six positive qualifications for the elder. The first is "hospitable" (Titus 1:8) and is the same word used in First Timothy 3:2. More details concerning this word can be viewed in the previous section on First Timothy. In the second, the elder must "love what is good" (Titus 1:8). The leader must be devoted to the good of mankind as well as creation itself. Thirdly, the overseer is "self-controlled" (Titus 1:8). The same word to describe this characteristic is found in the preceding section on First Timothy. This term conveys the idea of sensible or sober-minded. The leader considers situations and balances his next steps. He must have an excellent testimony with others in his dealings with them. Fourth, the leader must be "holy" (Titus 1:8). This word conveys the idea of being set apart and free from the blot of sin in his life. He is not sinless, for no man is, but keeps very short accounts with God and confesses sin. Without the finished work of Christ and the enabling power of the Spirit, none of these characteristics is attainable. Praise God for His gift to us! Fifth, we see that the elder must be "disciplined" (Titus 1:8). The idea conveyed here is one of self-control over areas of life that can pull the leader away from God. It does not mean that the shepherd has no pleasure or is joyless, but that he controls areas that could become harmful to self and others. Lastly, Titus is to appoint elders who "hold firmly to the trustworthy messages as it has been taught" (Titus 1:9). He must be true to the faith of the church and hold to doctrinal stability.

1 Peter 5:1-4

Peter was very concerned that the elders directing God's flock strive to be at their best. He devoted the last section of his letter to the subject of the elder in the local assembly. When hardships come to the flock, the members must look to the elders for direction and leadership. With these thoughts in mind, Peter shared these principles in First Peter 5:1-4.

In the first verse Peter established his credibility with his readers. He mentions the fact that he is a "witness of Christ's sufferings." From this phrase we get our English word for "martyr." A martyr is a witness who tells what he has seen and heard from an earlier time or event.

Since the shepherd/elder must be active in the equipping ministry through teaching by example, it follows that the shepherd must be involved in shepherding activities. The shepherd should be ready to serve the sheep of his flock. This should be done willingly, according to First Peter 5:2. Shepherding is one of the most desirable and gratifying areas of personal ministry. The shepherd has the great task of "watching over" the sheep. Peter stressed this point by the use of the aorist imperative *poimante*, indicating that it is something that needs to be done with increased action rather than routine. Peter warned against the idea of shepherding to make money, but instead to have a ready and eager mind as one shepherds the flock.

Inherent to the task of shepherding is the task of leadership. A leader is one who goes in front, setting the pace and inviting people to follow him. But it is very important that the shepherd not go too far out in front of the sheep. He must stay in touch with the sheep and keep them informed. He must also be a decisive leader and exercise the discipline of planning ahead.

Peter used the present participle *katakurieuontes* to describe the idea of "lording it over" the sheep. This type of legalistic behavior can overburden, confuse and divide the flock. Not "lording it over the sheep" is the final of the three contrasts Peter uses in verses two and three. Peter used (but....not) contrasts in the Greek to show that his disciples were to be servants and ministers, not bosses and executives.[5] The general idea from this passage is one of example, more specifically, the example of the shepherd who is walking closely with the Lord. The sheep look to the shepherd, and as the shepherd walks closely with the Lord, the flock will follow Him as well.

Verse four describes the reward that awaits the shepherd. When the "Chief Shepherd" appears (*parousia* or coming), the pastors or undershepherds will receive a reward. This crown will not wither but will consist of glory and honor. A very important relationship appears in verse four. Peter pointed out that the Chief Shepherd supersedes the authority of the shepherd/elder ministry. All shepherds must understand that they serve Christ who is the Chief! The emphasis of this verse should be one's faithfulness to the Lord. We will all appear before the Lord, and the desire of the faithful shepherd should be loving obedience to Jesus Christ.

Calling

We need to make sure that the shepherd is fit for ministry and has the call of God placed on his life for this task. I agree with E. Glenn Wagner who states that there must "be an unquenchable desire burning in the human heart to serve God in this way."[6] The desire for faithful service comes from within a man and is placed there by God. Below are questions that might help anchor this call in a person's life.

- ☞ Is there evidence that he practices spiritual disciplines in his life?

- ☞ Is there confirmation from a home church, formal training, a form of licensure and ordination to help establish this call to ministry?

- ☞ Has the man examined himself in light of the

characteristics found in God's Word concerning the call to ministry and qualifications?

☞ Does the person like people enough to give himself in service to them unselfishly?

☞ Is he able to relate meaningfully to people in all kinds of situations and, if needed, confront them lovingly?

☞ Is he a motivator who is able to inspire people to undertake even greater and more exciting tasks?

☞ Is he able to communicate well with people?

☞ Is he able to organize thoughts in a logical fashion and present a sermon or a lesson in such a way that people will follow the thoughts and do something about what they hear?

☞ Is he able to perform under stress?

☞ Is he a disciplined person and able to manage his time well so as to accomplish the many tasks of a shepherd?

These questions will help a man make this most interesting and rewarding journey toward being a faithful shepherd.

Biblical Tasks

Elder

Elders are men who satisfy the qualifications for the office of elder set forth in First Timothy 3:1–7 and

Titus 1:6–9. The church must recognize these men as gifted and willing to serve in this calling. They are received as gifts of Christ to His church and set apart as elders. Eldership is crucial to the sound health of a biblical congregation. David Dickson shares, "So necessary is the eldership for the superintendence of a congregation that practical wisdom would demand it even if Scripture did not provide it. In ordinary congregations it is physically impossible for the ministers to do all that is needful, or they must cease to give themselves to prayer and the ministry of the Word."[7] The elders oversee the ministry and resources of the church. In keeping with the principles set forth in Acts 6:1–7 and First Peter 5:1–4, elders should devote their time to prayer, the ministry of the Word (by teaching and encouraging sound doctrine) and shepherding God's flock. Rick Gregory states, "These godly men are set apart from within the congregation itself to provide humble, selfless leadership as they serve the Lord Jesus Christ as undershepherds to the flock of God – this is described as 'ruling' or 'leading' (1 Tim. 5:17; Heb. 13:7, 17)."[8]

Elders also oversee the work of the deacons and appointed church agents and committees, conduct worship services, oversee the ordinances of baptism and communion, equip the membership for the work of the ministry, encourage sound doctrine and practice, admonish and correct error, oversee the process of church discipline, coordinate and promote the ministries of the church and mobilize the church for world missions. Elders also ensure that all who minister the Word to the congregation share fundamental convictions.

Deacon

When it comes to deacon ministry, its heart is found in serving. The very word for deacon means "one who serves." Jesus was the ultimate example of servanthood as His mission was to be a servant (Mark 10:45).

Considering others better than yourself and honoring another above yourself are concepts and ideas that run counter to our culture and even many within the church. When we desire our own glory, our faith is hindered. The one who seeks his own glory is no longer seeking God or the good of his neighbor.

When it comes to my own attitudes, if my sinfulness appears in any way smaller or less offensive in comparison than the sins of others, I am not truly recognizing my sinfulness at all. Listen to the apostle Paul's emphatic statement concerning this in First Timothy 1:15: "Here is a trustworthy saying that deserves full acceptance: Christ Jesus came into the world to save sinners – of whom I am the worst." Understood correctly, this essential virtue of deacon ministry has to be its foundation, or the house on which it stands will be shaken by the shifting sands of cultural pressure to be "ones who lead" rather than "ones who serve."

Often leadership models in the church resemble business practices of the world. It comes from the American success ethic which puts such strong pressure upon the church. The first deacons were men who were primarily filled with the Spirit of God (Acts 6:3), not the spirit of the age. The office of deacon is described in First Timothy 3:8–13 and Acts 6:1–7.

The church must recognize men who are giving

of themselves in service to the body of believers and who possess particular gifts of service. These men are received as gifts of Christ to His church and set apart as deacons. Deacons and deaconesses care for the temporal needs of members, attend to the accommodations for public worship, and encourage and support those able to help others and those with gifts of administration. The following chart describes the deacon qualifications.

Biblical Qualifications for Deacon		
English Word/ Phrase	**Greek Word/ Phrase**	**Reference**
"respect"	*semnous*	1 Tim. 3:8
"sincere"	*me dilogous*	1 Tim. 3:8
"not indulging in much wine"	*me oino pollow prosexontas*	1 Tim. 3:8
"not pusuing dishonest gain"	*me aischrokerdeis*	1 Tim. 3:8
"keeps hold of deep truths of the faith with a clear conscience"	*musterion tes pisteuos en kathara suneidesei*	1 Tim. 3:9
"tested"	*dokimazesthosan*	1 Tim. 3:10

| "husband of but one wife" | *mias gunaikos andres* | 1 Tim. 3:12 |
| "manage his children and his household well" | *teknon kalous proistamenoi kai ton idion oikon* | 1 Tim. 3:12 |

Pastor

A friend contacted me recently and told me how he and his high school buddy were members of a team that won a national championship playing American Legion baseball. He recalled that it was fun to revisit those memories of winning the tournament but not as much fun as actually playing the game of baseball. I have similar feelings when explaining the tasks of a pastor. There is greater satisfaction for me to do the work than to talk about it. Nevertheless, the description of a pastor's work deserves a chapter of its own.

chapter three

The Pastor Shepherd

T HE BIBLICAL DESCRIPTION OF A PASTOR'S TASK is a wonderful study in itself. In keeping with the shepherding model presented in the last chapter, "pastor shepherd" is the appropriate title, given all that he does. As an elder, he satisfies the qualifications of First Timothy 3:1-7 and Titus 1:6-9. He is received as a gift of Christ to His church and set apart as an elder. But the church must recognize this man as particularly gifted and called to the full time ministry of preaching and teaching. The pastor shepherd is the one who trains leaders, prays, preaches, oversees the administration of the ordinances of baptism and communion and performs other duties that usually pertain to that office. Following are the top six duties of ministry a pastor shepherd should have.

CORRECTING

The work of the pastor is that of building up, not

tearing down. He should build on the foundation laid down by Jesus Christ. He must develop holiness and guard his character so that he is not a stumbling block to those who hear his preaching and teaching of the Word. The shepherd is a protector (John 10:11-14). As such, a pastor watches over the church and patiently corrects when it is in error.

The concept of correcting is difficult for some but must not be ignored by the pastor. The standard for all correction should be the Bible. During those times when correction takes place, the pastor should offer correction privately whenever possible. When the pastor is humble with correction, his comments will more likely be heard by the one being corrected. The whole event should be one of building up rather than tearing down. The pastor shepherd who fails to follow this careful course of correction will regret words and perhaps actions that damage instead of edify. Saying truthful words in love to one another is always good but may not be appropriate in public settings. On sensitive matters, saying them privately when possible is advisable to keep the bond of peace. Early in my ministry as a pastor, I failed to follow this advice on one occasion, and it disrupted the vital work of the church because of the pain it caused. Thank God for forgiveness, for in this situation, all is now forgiven. Sadly the learning process of the pastor shepherd can cause unnecessary harm. Be very careful, my brothers, to correct according to biblical standards because our errors deeply affect God's people (Matt. 18:15-20; Gal. 6:1-5).

Paul urged Timothy to use gentleness when correcting. "And the Lord's servant must not quarrel;

instead, he must be kind to everyone, able to teach, not resentful. Those who oppose him he must gently instruct, in the hope that God will grant them repentance leading them to a knowledge of the truth, and that they will come to their senses and escape from the trap of the devil, who has taken them captive to do his will" (2 Tim. 2:24-26). Correcting is a test of the pastor's character as much as it is a defining moment for the one being corrected.

EQUIPPING

The shepherd is an elder who trains the flock in the church. His immediate purpose is to prepare the saints for ministry. What would it be like if our president declared that our nation was at war but failed to ask for citizens to fill the ranks of the military or to provide those who do with any weapons to carry out the conflict and engage the enemy in battle? Our reaction to this scenario might be a mixture of disbelief and fear. Yet, we put up with this kind of leadership in some of our churches. Pastors may not convey the fact that a spiritual battle is taking place, let alone provide instruction on how to use the "whole armor of God" (Eph. 6:13-17).

It is the shepherd's duty "to prepare God's people for works of service, so that the body of Christ may be built up (Eph. 4:12). For "built up," Paul uses the Greek word *katartismos*, a medical term that describes the setting of bones and conveys the image of restoring to original condition.[1]

Sunday after Sunday the saints should be instructed so that they are built up through the power of the

Word of God (2 Tim. 3:16-17), prayer (Acts 6:4), testing (Jam. 1:2-4) and suffering (1 Pet. 5:10). A benefit from equipping God's people is that the body will be built up. The church has direction from the Lord to be built up through His Word (Acts 20:32). Once I was asked to teach a weekly Bible study at the home of an elderly widow who lived in the country. She gathered her neighbors, and we met for an hour and a half each week for a year. Those times of teaching God's Word, praying and sharing in their personal lives produced wonderful results. At the conclusion of that year, a church was developed from the attenders and is strong to this day. When God speaks to His people through the Word, tremendous developments will be set in motion.

The great objective for the church is to become mature. Paul said that the church must equip the saints "for works of service, so that the body of Christ may be built up until we all reach unity in the faith and in the knowledge of the Son of God and become mature, attaining to the whole measure of the fullness of Christ" (Eph. 4:13).

Equipping God's people for service and building them up develop unity in the body of Christ. The church should strive to achieve unity in the faith and knowledge of the Son of God. Our knowledge of the Son of God must be full and complete (Phil. 3:8-10, 12) and is part of the sanctification process for the believer.

The following diagram provides a visual picture of areas where equipping takes place through the ministry of the church. Equipping is done through morning worship (celebration); home groups, Sunday school classes and Adult Bible Fellowship (congregation);

discipleship groups (cell) and one-on-one (core). In these ways, the whole body is built up in love so that the church grows up in Christ.

Local Church Ministry

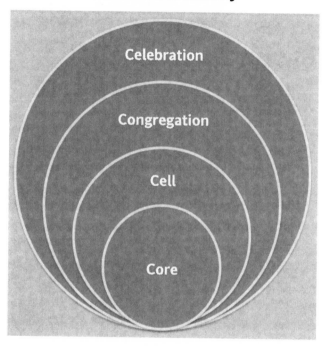

- ☛ **Celebration:** *The church body looking up to Christ in worship and to the Word for motivation.*

- ☛ **Congregation:** *Groups within the church where you know each other and where someone is missed when he or she is not there. They are organized for fellowship, study and growth, and outreach.*

- ☞ *Cell:* *Small groups made up of seven to twelve people where there is growing intimacy and discipleship.*

- ☞ *Core:* *One-on-one discipleship, accountability, mentoring; a place where oneness and spiritual training take place.*

LEADING

Images flood our minds of men and women throughout history who have achieved merit in the arena of leadership. Leadership isn't always the man going before his troops or the woman bent over a patient's bed providing medical assistance. Leadership is, however, going in advance of others in war or healthcare or any other situation where individuals take charge. It is also being an active listener, empowering others to do a task, coaching, taking charge, inspiring others and much more. A leader finds his or her sweet spot in developing others, having a positive influence on others, motivating others and communicating information for the good of others. The pastor shepherd has this kind of leadership in the church. Pastors have people entrusted to their care in a similar way that a father has with his family. Peter provided a striking contrast in leading when he said that a leader should not be described as one "lording it over those entrusted to you, but being examples to the flock" (1 Pet. 5:3).

Pastors need to give great care to their leadership. Pastoral leadership is to be strong yet gentle and often just moments apart. I enjoy watching Olympic athletes in paired figure skating events. The man appears strong as he lifts his female partner in the air, and the next moment he is very gentle as he eases her landing on the ice. That is a picture of strength under control. Leadership is like that.

Leaders may have the ability to stand in front of a crowd of people, encouraging them to move forward from their stationary positions, and still have the patience to listen and then help one person go from Point A to Point B in their life journey. Don't think of listening as passive. A leader who listens well knows what to do with what he has heard. He has turned listening into an art form with eternal value.

A pastor has to be a leader. It is imperative that he has vision and can communicate goals and dreams. Pastors need to know when to push a major concept in the church and when to back away. If no one is behind you when you are leading, you have lost your people. So leaders may need to adjust their speed when it comes to leadership objectives and goals. Leading is not just dreaming up the next big event but helping the people of the church come up with the next big event. As a leader you are moving toward a goal, arm in arm with those you lead.

PRAYING

While leading might get a pastor's name in the headlines, the praying pastor often has no such fanfare. The praying pastor finds expression in humbly and reverently calling out to God on behalf of the sheep. Praying is going into battle, spiritually speaking, for the souls of people and the needs of the saints. This kind of prayer takes discipline. It is hard work. I confess that some of my pastoral prayer times have been less than "powerful and effective" (Jam. 5:16). This is usually a result of the lack of self-discipline. I have to watch my schedule in order to get proper amounts of sleep and exercise, while keeping other activities in check if I aim to have a proper prayer life.

From concerns about false teachers, Paul turned his attention to the church in First Timothy 2. He began with what he considered most important: prayer. What often comes last in a church's priorities should actually come first. Paul urged "then, first of all, that requests, prayers, intercession and thanksgiving be made for everyone" (1 Tim. 2:1). The praying pastor seeks communion with God. He makes petition for the people in his care. As the leader of a particular flock, he prays for the will of God to be accomplished in and through the sheep of his care. As a pastor intercedes for the people, he expresses a childlike confidence before the Lord. Prayer is also a time of thanking God for the blessings to His saints.

Consider adding to your library the four-volume set on all the prayers in the Bible written by Jim Rosscup.[2] This will be hours of worthwhile reading that you will not regret. Select some of the prayers of Paul in his epistles. This is an especially good way to pray for those you shepherd and love. Here's how it works. Insert the name of the one for whom you are praying when you come to a personal pronoun in the text of the prayer. I will use my wife's name as an example. "For this reason I kneel before the Father, from whom his whole family in heaven and on the earth derives its name. I pray that out of his glorious riches he may strengthen (Melody) with power through his Spirit in (Melody's) inner being, so that Christ may dwell in (Melody's) heart through faith. And I pray that (Melody), being rooted and established in love, may have power, together with all the saints, to grasp how wide and long and high and deep is the love of Christ, and to know this love that surpasses knowledge – that (Melody) may be filled to the measure of all the fullness of God" (Ephesians 3:14-19).

We tried this method of prayer in a small group setting at the church I currently pastor. In pairs, people prayed for one another using a prayer out of Scripture. After hearing his partner pray for him, one man commented, "That prayer was exactly what I needed." The wording was perfect for his situation. A woman shared, "I feel powerful and effective when using words from God's Word. How could you pray amiss?"

PREACHING AND TEACHING

Paul wrote to the believers in Rome asking "How, then, can they call on the one they have not believed in? And how can they believe in the one of whom they have not heard? And how can they hear without someone preaching to them?" (Rom. 10:14). About six years later, Paul wrote to Timothy exhorting the young pastor to "preach the Word; be prepared in season and out of season; correct, rebuke and encourage – with great patience and careful instruction" (2 Tim. 4:2). Years ago a revival service was held at a church I pastored in Ohio. God used it to teach me that the inspired Bible demands an inspired ministry. Uninspired preachers and teachers – those who rest on their own strengths rather than rely on God – can quench the fire of heaven when it touches their unprepared tongues. On the contrary, it was amazing to see how God used our speaker during those services. At the end of the last sermon, well over twenty percent of the people responded to the altar call. Tears of joy fell and lives were changed because hearts were broken and wrongs were made right. The speaker had learned that inspiration inspires. It is simply useless for us to claim that the Bible is inspired and not share in its inspiration. In His strength we need to read and teach the Bible with our whole hearts as if lives depended on the message. Spiritual fire from heaven falls upon the prepared material of the preacher who relies on God. His words make their mark, and lives are changed to the glory of God. Peter's sermon just after Pentecost shows this kind of effect (Acts 2:37).

Titus was urged by Paul to "hold fast" *(antecho)* to the faithful Word (Titus 1:4). The pastor must preach and teach, exhort, expound the Word at any time, correct and refute error. Pastors who are not doing these things are missing the mark.

One of the main duties of the pastor is instruction surrounding the Word of God. Pastors must preach and teach. As a seminary student many years ago, I was leaving church after morning worship with my wife. We were met at the door by an aged man who extended his hand to me and said, "Now that you are a pastor, you need to be able to preach, pray or die on a moment's notice." I have never forgotten those words. That is the life of a pastor, to preach and pray. I am still waiting on the "die" part and ready to go any time the Lord calls.

SHEPHERDING

Using the metaphor of a shepherd to describe a pastor makes a beautiful picture. It is one of the most honoring and humbling tributes a person can pay a pastor. When the shepherd imagery comes to mind, some might visualize a very pastoral and quiet scene. On the other hand, one might imagine bad smells and unruly animals. I trust your image of the shepherd is somewhere between the two extremes.

Just who is the shepherd? Is the shepherd of the flock the pastor? What about the concept of overseer? Just where does the elder come into the picture? These are all good questions, and Peter provided us with a New Testament understanding of the shepherd. "To the elders *(presbuteros)* among you, I appeal as a fellow elder *(sumpresbuteros)*, a witness of Christ's sufferings and one who also will share in the glory to be revealed: Be shepherds *(poimanate)* of God's flock that is under your care, serving as overseers *(episkopountes)* – not because you must, but because you are willing, as God wants you to be; not greedy for money, but eager to serve" (1 Pet. 5:1-2). The shepherd is elder, pastor and overseer. All three Greek words are used interchangeably to describe the shepherd.

Jesus is a shepherd "I am the good shepherd. The good shepherd lays down his life for the sheep." (John 10:11) He commands His servant-leaders to be shepherds. He sees individual people as His sheep. However, the shepherd model is in danger of being eliminated because of the corporate community model that has permeated our churches.[3]

The shepherd has concern for the sheep. He provides rest and keeps watch over the sheep for security and protection. The shepherd takes the sheep to fresh grazing land and provides refreshment and healing when necessary. This is what the shepherd does. The term "pastor" means shepherd. The pastor is one who leads by example in carrying out the equipping ministry Paul describes in Ephesians 4:11-16. He gives guidance and leadership along with personal fellowship, loving friendship and encouragement. If you want to encourage your pastor and brighten his day, just thank him for being your pastor shepherd. Those words will be affirmation to your shepherd and are sure to brighten his day.

Gordon MacDonald commented on these qualities recently by writing about the apostle Paul:

> As I made my way through Paul's letters, I saw, once again, that he was a missionary-apostle (church planter), a theologian, a developer of leaders. But most important, Paul was a shepherd-pastor. He clearly understood – like the shepherd of Psalm 23 – the significance of congregational feeding and protection. Here's how Paul practiced what he preached about guarding the flock. Affirming: quick to identify evidences of God's work in persons and people; Thankful: ready to express gratitude for any act of generosity; Corrective: never reluctant to identify sin and rebuke it; Prophetic: warning of consequences if people were bent on making

bad choices; Instructive: enlarging the theological base of people's faith; Protective: quick to defend those who were vulnerable; Transparent: unashamed to speak of his own weaknesses and sins; Affectionate: anxious for people to know how much he loved them; Prayerful: frequently praying 'aloud' in his letters for people and their needs; Developmental: identifying, raising up those who might become leaders; Observable: presenting a model of the Christ-following life that others could copy.[4]

As a shepherd I will do this willingly according to First Peter 5:2. Shepherding is one of the most desirable and gratifying areas of Christian ministry for those who are called to it. Charles Jefferson notes, "The age of the shepherd has just arrived. Never has he been so much needed as now."[5]

"Every true Christian ought to be a man of prayer. All his views, all his affections, all his desires, hopes and joys, ought to be constantly mounting on the wings of devotions, and flying before him into heaven."

John Smith, *Lectures on the Nature and End of the Sacred Office* (Baltimore: A. Neal, 1810), 33.

"Faith is the first act of the regenerated soul; and the most important act, for it draws all holy affections in its train. But though it sweetly mingles with every other grace, it is distinct from them all. It is firm persuasion of belief of the truth, apprehended under the illumination of the Holy Spirit."

Archibald Alexander, *Thoughts on Religious Experience* (Philadelphia: Presbyterian Board of Publication, 1844), 86.

part two

Keys to Success

"Hope and fasting are said to be the true wings of prayer. Fasting is but the wing of a bird; but hope is like the wing of an angel soaring up to heaven, and bears our prayers to the throne of grace."

Jeremy Taylor, *Rules and Exercises of Holy Living* (London: Bell and Daldy Fleet Street, 1857), 237.

"Meditation and prayer are the daily exercise and delight of a devout and pious soul. In meditation we converse with ourselves in prayer we converse with God; and what converse can we desire more agreeable and more advantageous."

Matthew Henry, *Communicant's Companion* (New York: L. and F. Lockwood, 1819), 107.

chapter four

Core Spiritual Disciplines

LIFE IS A JOURNEY, AND PEOPLE CHANGE OVER time as they are on that journey. It is safe to say that one is not the same as he or she was ten years ago. Imagine a twenty-two-year-old acting like a twelve-year-old! As people face issues in life and grow older, change occurs. Hopefully, one matures and grows stronger as life goes on.

Talk to a couple with a strong marriage. They will tell you that they have changed over the years as they learned more about each other and sought to support and encourage each other. As they lived together and had to deal with a variety of life issues, their marriage grew and matured.

Ask most parents today if they were truly up to the task when their first child was born, and they would say, an emphatic, "No!" In fact, each stage of a child's development presents new challenges. The parents of a newborn believe that they will never sleep again. Eventually they get to sleep through the night until their children become teenagers and are driving. Once again the parents are not sleeping, but this time for different reasons. Because children have different personalities, good parents adapt in order to effectively parent their children. The parents grow and mature as their children grow.

On the other hand, when many people consider their spiritual life, they believe it is accomplished as a single point. Either one is spiritual or one is not. Either one is saved or one is not. I have met many people who rattle off some decision they made at some point in their childhood. Because of that one-time event, they do not see the need to continue to grow spiritually. Others are not willing to commit to God because they believe that before they can be right with God, they must have a certain level of knowledge or be living a certain type of life. Because they are not at such a point, they reject the things of God. Either extreme is unhealthy.

A healthy way to look at spiritual life is to regard it as a journey. This journey is best described as the deepening of a personal relationship with God through His Son, Jesus Christ. Such a journey is a process that can be more relational than rule-oriented. M. Robert Mulholland writes,

When God puts a 'finger' on those things in our lives which are inconsistent for God's will for our wholeness, it is not simply to point them out. It is not just to say that they must go or must be changed. That finger has a hand attached that offers us nurture into wholeness which we need at that point.[1]

Such a journey invites people to be relational with God as well as with others. It is easier to invite others to walk with us. Traveling together allows the companions to track where they are and anticipate what the next steps will be in spiritual formation.

The activities individuals engage in shape their spiritual formation. What those activities are becomes the big question. Do we lean toward the natural or the spiritual man of whom Paul spoke in First Corinthians 15:44-49? Make it your goal to conform to the image of Christ in every way by praying daily for the Spirit's help and direction. As Mulholland writes, "Genuine spiritual formation brings about a radical shift from being our own production to being God's workmanship."[2]

Paul wrote in First Timothy 4:7 that discipline is the secret to godliness. This word "discipline" seems to have disappeared from our culture, since modern America hardly knows what it means. Without discipline, there is no other way to attain godliness. Thankfully, the power to be faithful and to lead a disciplined life is found in the Holy Spirit.

In First Timothy 4:7-8, Paul used the Greek word *gumnaze,* a present imperative that means "keep on exercising." The verb is derived from the adjective *gumnos* (naked) denoting the practice of an athlete removing clothing in order to exercise. Our English words of gym and gymnasium find their derivation from this Greek verb. Christians must exercise spiritually toward godliness. The difference between physical and spiritual exercise can be found in the Greek phrase *pros oligon* that means "for a little." The benefits of gymnastic exercise last only for a little while. Spiritual exercise brings eternal benefits.

Christians need to ask themselves these questions: Are we godly? What hinders us? What can we do about it? There is only one possible way to go about it. Christians must become disciplined toward godliness until we do in fact become godly in character. No "magic formula" is involved. There must be desire, and the grace of God does the rest.

It is imperative that we understand the meaning of grace. In a deeper way than ever before, understanding came to me through the phrase, "Preach the gospel to yourself everyday." Written in big letters inside the front cover of my Bible, this was the challenge given by Jerry Bridges in a seminary class of mine several years ago. He explained, "...if we are going to preach the gospel to ourselves every day and learn to live by it, we need to understand Romans 3:19-26."[3] In this passage the world is condemned and the Righteous One is revealed through the act of justification as we are declared righteous in His sight. Preaching the gospel to yourself daily expresses how thankful we are for His mercy and grace. As believing Christians, we know this is true, but preaching the gospel daily means that we are saying it with heart-felt gratitude for the redemption we have in Christ. Over time, the reality of this short phrase has made a difference in my actions, words, ethics, morality and more. Our biblical worldview can be transformed by the fact that we believe this phrase and daily express it back to God in gratitude.

Core Spiritual Disciplines

Core spiritual disciplines (CSDs) in the life of a believer are essential for the journey of spiritual life. These practices that connect the believer to God, activities such as confession, prayer, study and worship, are spiritual nourishment. Just as nutrients from the food that is eaten are assimilated into the physical body for growth, development and wellness, spiritual disciplines build the believer's body into maturity, wholeness and holiness. Spiritual disciplines show their greatest personal worth when they are incorporated into the daily events of our lives.

Core spiritual disciplines are not new. The Bible is filled with example after example of disciplines and their practice. Consider the early church. Is it any wonder the early church grew so much, as recorded in the book of Acts? Think of the extraordinary impact the Christian community could have on the world today if CSDs were practiced more! Fresh obedience to the old truths is the need of the hour.

In recent years numerous books have been written about spiritual disciplines. Obviously, the numbers and categories of the disciplines vary among the authors. Jan Johnson lists sixteen spiritual disciplines and adds, "Many other activities become spiritual disciplines for us as we practice them on a regular basis."[4] R. Kent Hughes claims that there are "...sixteen disciplines which are essential to a godly life."[5] Adele Calhoun contributes to the study of spiritual disciplines by sharing sixty-two disciplines.[6] Dallas Willard looks at fifteen spiritual disciplines that "... make an especially important contribution to spiritual growth."[7] Ruth Haley Barton lists twenty-two spiritual disciplines that correspond to the needs of leaders.[8] Stephen Macchia claims that there are five spiritual disciplines that are essential to the relationship between the believer and Christ.[9]

All the spiritual disciplines mentioned or implied in Scripture cannot be examined in detail here. Instead, this book will develop eight disciplines as CSDs for the life of the believer. These are listed and defined on the following chart in alphabetical order and not necessarily in order of importance. The very brief summaries that follow cannot do justice to the depths of teaching that each CSD could contain, but will perhaps whet the reader's appetite to examine them more closely.

Core Spiritual Discipline Definitions	
Confession	Agreeing with God that He is right about a particular matter and that the offenders are wrong.
Fasting	The voluntary act of being without food or other things and is usually a response to mourning over sin.
Life Together	Engaging in the body life of believing Christians for biblical support in a variety of locations.
Prayer	Coming into the presence of God and speaking to Him.

Core Spiritual Disciplines

Service	Meeting practical needs or performing tasks for others.
Silence	Removing oneself from people, places or things in order to hear God.
Study	Reading, interpreting and applying what is read to one's life.
Worship	Our response and praise to God.

CONFESSION

This discipline may be the most difficult discipline to practice because we have to admit that we are wrong. Through the act of confession, believers agree with God that He is right and what they did was wrong (Ps. 66:18). Declaring our guilt may be the hardest thing to do, but confession is a requirement for obedient living.

John wrote in First John 1:8-10 to individuals influenced by gnostic false teachers who denied personal responsibility for sin. In fact, these teachers maintained they were sinless and unable to sin in the future. But believers cannot deny the presence of sin in their lives (1 John 1:8), the cure for sin (1 John 1:9) or the practice of sin (1 John 1:10). To be without sin is not possible for believers, "for all have sinned and fall short of the glory of God" (Rom. 3:23). Declaring that we have not sinned makes God out to be untruthful when

He has already taken pity on sinful mankind (1 John 1:10). He sent His Son, Jesus Christ, as the needed Savior. Without the shedding of His blood (1 John 1:7), no believer can be pure and spotless before God (1 Pet. 1:18-20). We agree with God that Christ paid for sin in full (Rom. 5:8-10). Therefore, when we humble ourselves in the discipline of confession, God's promises of forgiveness and cleansing are ours (1 John 1:9).

Confession and self-examination work together to begin the restoration process of the believer, and God's grace becomes real. The author of Proverbs declared that when sin is confessed, mercy is found (Prov. 28:13). In practicing confession, the heart is searched so that the inner man, along with the sin, are exposed (Heb. 4:12). After all, nothing is hidden from the sight of God (Heb. 4:13), and all Christians will stand before Jesus to give an account (Rom. 14:10-12).

Righteousness is completely fulfilled in God both in respect to what He does and who He is. So confession is a picture of waking up to the facts of who we are as natural men and who we will become as spiritual men by seeing who God is.

When Christians truly understand what sin has done to God, to others and themselves, they will have sorrow that leads to repentance by way of confession. Paul stated to Ephesian believers that confession is also an act of the will, a turning away or repentance from the wrong that hurt God (Eph. 4:30).

FASTING

Fasting is the voluntary act of going without food or other things. It may be total or partial abstinence for a limited time for spiritual benefit. This CSD is undertaken for spiritual reasons, not dietary (in the case of abstinence from food). Recently I spoke with a group of high school guys at the church I pastor and asked them, "What are your thoughts about fasting?" The response to my question was instant silence. With a little coaxing, they began to respond. One young man stated, "Every time I hear the word fasting, it makes me mad." Encouraging him to expand on that statement, he said "I like food and don't want to starve." This is an honest answer, and who can blame him for the response? None of us like going without food very long.

As I looked deeper into the practice of fasting, some surprising discoveries surfaced. My research uncovered an extra-biblical account that encouraged fasting in the New Testament church.[10] As a manual of instruction to the early Christians, the *Didache* was a guide to believers desiring to be part of the church. This window on the earliest of Christian communities showed that fasting was held in high regard.

There are also many instances in the Bible where fasting is described. In First Samuel 7:2-13 the Jewish people were encouraged to cease their idolatry (1 Sam. 7:3-4) and gather together at Mizpah (1 Sam. 7:5). This assembly was for national repentance. Fasting on this occasion was a process leading to purification and humbling of themselves before God. The ceremony was interrupted by the attack of the Philistines, but God came to the aid of Israel, and the attackers fled in panic (1 Sam. 7:5-11).

A time of fasting in David's life is described in the first chapter of Second Samuel. In this passage David is informed that the Philistines had routed the army of Israel in battle, and Saul and his sons had died in the conflict (2 Sam. 1:1-10). Upon hearing this news, David and his men mourned, wept and fasted for a period of time (2 Sam. 1:11-12).

Nehemiah recorded that fasting, confession of sin and reading the Law of Moses all took place in accordance with prescribed feasts observed by Israel (Neh. 9). These feasts were to acknowledge God's mercy and judgments. At the close of this observance, the Israelites were to renew their promises to God (Neh. 9:38).

Jonah provided the account of the people at Nineveh who responded to the message of God that was delivered to them (Jonah 3). As a response to this message, the king of Nineveh declared a fast that was brought on by repentance and humility on account of the sins of Nineveh (Jonah 3:7-8). This must have been very powerful preaching by Jonah when the entire city turned from sin to God. The response of the Ninevites was humility, repentance, mourning and fasting.

A window into the life of Jesus presents another image of fasting (Matthew 4). His first act of ministry after being baptized was to have an appointment with Satan surrounding temptation (Matt. 4:1-11). But it was not without preparation, for the fasting of Jesus began forty days before the conflict with Satan occurred. A similar example of this extended length of fasting can be seen in the Old Testament from the life of Elijah (1 Kings 19:18). Likewise, Moses fasted forty days before receiving the law of God (Ex. 34:28). Paul provided understanding of these incredible feats of fasting when he wrote "For the kingdom of God is not a matter of eating and drinking, but of righteousness, peace and joy in the Holy Spirit" (Rom. 14:17).

Fasting to determine the will of God may be implied by the Scripture but it is nowhere explicitly stated as a reason for fasting. It can be said that fasting increases the awareness of the believer who longs for the will of God. James encouraged, "If any of you lacks wisdom, he should ask of God, who gives generously to all without finding fault, and it will be given to Him" (Jas 1:5). Prayer is one of the best ways to know God's will.

Fasting is a response that indicates mourning over sin (Deut. 9:15-18; 1 Kings 21:17-29; Dan. 9:3-5). It is seen as an expression of grief when danger was upon individuals (2 Chron. 20:3; Neh. 1:4; Esther 4:3, 16). Fasting was common to the Jewish people on the Day of Atonement (Lev. 16:29-31; 23:26-32; Num. 29:7). When Jesus preached the Sermon on the Mount (Matt. 6:16-18) He spoke of fasting and even taught the disciples to fast (Matt. 9:14-17; Mark 2:18-20; Luke 5:33-39). The early church practiced fasting and often combined it with prayer (Acts 13:1-3; 14:21-23). The apostle Paul spoke about fasting and practiced it (2 Cor. 6:4-10; 11:23-28). It was practiced by our Lord and is a CSD the present-day church should continue.

This discipline is not for the faint of heart, but for the person who desires to do business with God. That business is seeking God's face in cleansing the heart of sin. Fasting is not for public display (Matt. 6:16-18), nor is it to be practiced routinely without reason (Matt. 9:14-17).

The silence of the group of high school guys is a pretty common response when asked about fasting. In my observation, the church is also silent on the practice of this discipline. But fasting is a powerful weapon in the arsenal of the believer to do battle with Satan and draw upon the incredible power of our awesome God!

LIFE TOGETHER

This spiritual discipline centers on the concept of Christians engaging in the community of believers around them. Participation in community shows the world what God's love is like. Mulholland writes, "When God begins to work with us at the deep levels of our incompleteness and brokenness, our bondage and sin, we need the body of Christ to support, encourage, challenge and nurture us toward wholeness...."[11] As Christians engage with one another in the body life of the church, one can see change and maturing take place in the lives of individuals. Mark Driscoll and Gerry Breshears describe what community should look like:

> The church obeys the Great Commandment to love. The church is supposed to be a Spirit-empowered loving community that devotes itself to fellowship. God's people live together in intentional relational community to seek the well being of one another in every way – physical, mental, spiritual, material, and emotional. This does not mean that everyone is required to be best friends with everyone else, but it does

mean that people take care of each other like extended family.[12]

Sadly, there are times when the world sees how badly Christians treat one another. Unwed mothers and divorced people often feel the brunt of such treatment. It has been said, "Christians are the only army in the world that kill their wounded."

It has been my observation over the years to see some Christians resist going to church on Sundays. The reasons vary. Some say a particular church might be lacking in a ministry program, preaching might not be to their liking, or numbers of a particular age group in the church might be too few to meet their needs, to mention a few. My sense in this matter is that people are trying to guard themselves from the gaze of God upon their lives. Sometimes we hide behind excuses to justify our absence from Church. They have a strong tendency to try to control situations in life, some even life itself. Resisting the ministry of the Church and the gathering of the Body of Christ allows people to maintain control. Mulholland warns, "Without a holistic corporate spirituality, there is a powerful tendency to become heterodox or heretical. Corporate spirituality is essential because privatization always fashions a spirituality that in some way allows us to maintain control of God.[13]

We Christians have difficulty going very deep with one another because it is in that experience of mutual openness where God does the crucifying work of nurturing us into wholeness (Gal. 2:20). The concept of life together moves against the flow of society that urges us to live privately, keep to ourselves and not get involved too deeply with people. Sunday after Sunday I attempt to reach the exit door of the church after the sermon has ended in order to greet people. Invariably, several from the congregation are gone before I am able to get there. Some Christians just resist getting close to others. Reasons for this vary, too, but I believe the fear of allowing others to see who we really are before God is a primary motivation for this behavior. Being a Christian is not just for Sunday morning church, but especially when believers are at home or in a community setting. As Christians live for Him, they proclaim Him wherever they are. Dietrich Bonheoffer shared that "...spiritual love proves itself in that everything it says and does commends Christ."[14]

Paul wrote to the church gathered in Rome (Rom. 12:9-12) to address the division between Jews and Gentiles. Harmony within the church depends on mutual love for fellow believers and devotion to God. The believer is to be "committed to the way of goodness; his whole life is wrapped up in it ('glued' to it)."[15] Paul exhorted believers in verse eleven not to be idle in any service, but to be earnest in all you do and to serve the Lord. John Murray writes about how "...dismal would tribulation be without hope and how defeatist would we be in persecution without the resources of hope and patience conveyed to us through prayer."[16] Paul ends this section of Scripture with the exhortation to contribute to the needs of believers and to practice hospitality.

It is important to understand that when Christians gather as a community, it is not to be exclusively at church. We engage in community when we want to grow spiritually in Christ. This community experience is everywhere and cannot be confined to one place. Life together needs to be embraced when the church gathers to look up in worship and to the Word for motivation. Groups may meet in homes where individuals are known and when someone is missed if not there. Christians should meet in small groups where there is growing intimacy and discipleship. Another place believers should meet for spiritual training is in one-on-one discipleship, accountability and mentoring.

The power of the group experience provides opportunity for dialogue and discussion. Small groups are the place where spiritual formation happens. The sanctuary is very suitable for celebration, but life together and community are realized in the power of the group experience.

PRAYER

The church I currently pastor is situated in a rich agricultural area so that the view out my office window is one of lush grass seed fields. Recently, I was praying in my office early on a Sunday morning before people arrived at church. The quiet solitude of my personal prayer time was broken by noise and activity outside the church. As I opened the blinds of my office window and looked out into the early morning darkness, I was able to see a farmer unloading sheep in a nearby field for grazing. I smiled at the sight and resumed my privilege of praying for the sheep that would soon be coming to church to be fed.

One of the most important disciplines for the

Christian to learn and practice is the art of prayer. Prayer is described as coming into the presence of God (Heb. 4:16). Picture the throne of grace as the place where God and man meet. We must humbly come up to the throne, an action which implies faith in the truth of sacrifice. Mulholland explains, "Prayer becomes a sacrificial offering of ourselves to God, to become God's agents of God's presence and action in the daily events and situations of our lives."[17]

Prayer is speaking to God and allowing God to communicate back to us (Phil. 4:6-7). Prayer brings peace from God to the believer that is seen in opposition to anxiety. It is in seeing God that we see the emptiness of what the world has to offer us. The process of reading Scripture, praying to God and pursuing moments of silence before Him provides blessing and joy in God's presence. Francois Fenelon stated, "Prayer is so necessary and the source of so much good, that the soul which has found this treasure cannot resist returning to it when left to itself."[18] When believers ask God to meet their needs, and He does, it is uplifting! The Christian life comes alive when believers see Him do mighty things in answer to their prayers.

In some form or another, prayer is a universal experience. A possible exception to this might be the atheist. But the Christian's prayer differs from all others in that it glorifies the Lord, and He is worthy of our praise (John 14:13). The goal of any prayer should be to bring glory to God the Father.

In addition to glorifying God and adoring Christ, the various aspects of prayer include confession (acknowledging sin before God), petition or supplication (making requests), thanksgiving (thanking

Him for His goodness and blessings) and intercession (requests for others). Intercession turns the believer's attention outward to make Christ known to those outside the Christian community. This is an act of prayer by which the people of God become incorporated into the world. The following diagram provides a visible picture of the aspects of prayer.

When Christians pray, their love is increased for those who are difficult to love (Luke 6:27-28). In fact, prayer is a powerful influence in the lives of those around us. Dallas Willard shares,

And here, finally, is the basic answer to the urgent need we all feel to influence others for good. That answer is prayer, asking God. This is the sure way in which the good that we can accomplish in others can be accomplished. Our confidence in God is the only thing that makes it possible to treat others as they should be treated. Hence we must look yet again at the 'therefore.' Having made clear the power of prayer to achieve the good ends we desire, Jesus says, 'Therefore, whatever you would like others to do to you, do that to them.' That is, because the power of asking and prayer is what it is, treat others as you would like to be treated.[19]

Concerning prayer, David Hansen writes, "In faith we believe that Jesus has truly overcome the world; in prayer we seek to know, through the gloom, the face we so long to see. Long prayer is faith's practical vehicle for our long journey to penetrate much darkness."[20]

We are called to pray at all times (Acts 6:4). We can pray when no other person is around or in the company of others. The point is, we need to pray. We need to be deliberate in our communication with God. Prayer should be woven into the fabric of daily life for the believer.

SERVICE

Meeting practical needs and performing tasks or responsibilities for others are the ideas behind service. Serving others involves humility, submission, surrender and sacrifice and is best characterized by the life of the Savior (Luke 22:27).

Service shows the relational aspect of Christianity where active participation takes place on behalf of others. Luke spoke of serving tables (Acts 6:1-3), John spoke of waiting at meals (John 2:5-9), Martha demonstrated the preparations of a hostess in Luke 10:40 and Paul spoke of collecting an offering (2 Cor. 8:19-20). Jesus washed the disciples' feet and asked them to follow His example (John 13:1-17). Jesus is the greatest example of service on the behalf of others when He came as God's servant to be our ransom (Mark 10:45). He freed mankind from the heavy weight and bondage of sin (Rom. 5:12). The Savior took our place on the cross to pay the penalty that mankind could not pay (Rom. 6:20).

The CSD of service is also a spiritual gift (1 Cor. 12) and a qualification for the deacon ministry (1 Tim. 3:8-13). Serving God in the church is an indicator that one is a recipient of His grace and that God is relating to mankind (Eph. 2:8-10). When believers minister to one another, they build up the body of Christ in the church (Eph. 4:11-12). This building up of the body generates edification among the saints making them stable believers (Eph. 4:11-16). As servants, then, Christians are not bystanders watching life, but they are actively involved in ministry toward others for the glory of God. They serve other people in ways that bring glory to Him.

Dallas Willard describes service as the "...high road to freedom from bondage to other people (Col. 3:22-24)."[21] As such, it "...allows us the freedom of humility that carries no burden of appearance."[22] Warren Wiersbe adds, "Serving God isn't punishment; it's nourishment."[23]

SILENCE

Quiet. Do you hear it? Silence is not something the average person seeks. Instead, thousands of images, sounds and activities fill our lives and compete for our attention. We have grown accustomed to life in a state of hyper stimulation. Frankly, I'm ready to revolt! I long to get off this roller coaster of noise and activity. Constant noise and perpetual activity can cause deep anxiety in the lives of over-stimulated people and to those around them.

The Psalmist said, "Be still and know that I am God..." (Ps. 46:10). This statement is a picture of contrast to our world today. The world is filled with noise countered with God's stillness. The world teaches people to multi-task to a greater degree than ever before, and to be silent goes the opposite direction. The Hebrew word for "be still" in Psalm 46:10 is a command to "...let go and let God do the work."[24] It is important to be reminded of how great God is. Ruth Haley Barton shares that through "...silence we give up control and allow God to be God in our life rather than being a thought in our head or an illustration in a sermon."[25]

The CSD of silence concerns itself with unplugging from something else in order to plug into God. When the noise of life is reduced, we hear Him. Believers who bring silence into their lives provide God with the opportunity to speak and communicate. In this way, silence offers the platform for an audience with God.

Practicing the CSD of silence provides time for me to reflect on my interactions with others. Silence helps me think through the words I have used in conversation and the actions that have played out in my life through different events. Consequently, more acceptable words and greater actions are fruits of silence, so that the next encounter with someone will be more Christ-honoring.

Silence is a challenge to every addiction in life. As silence is embraced in our lives, we begin to yield our lives to His control more and more. Silence causes me to see more of God and less of me. On the other hand, modern technology tends to lock up personalities and the ways people relate to one another. As a result, current society seems to be characterized by non-relationships. Everything, from smart phones to high definition television and all the techno gadgets in between, keeps people isolated from one another and from God. Barton shares "…all the forces of evil band together to prevent our knowing God in this way, because it brings to an end the dominion of those powers in our lives."[26]

Practicing this discipline is a way of paying attention to the Spirit of God and what He brings to the forefront of your mind. Try going to a quiet place soon, and take nothing but your Bible. When you get to that spot of solitude, quiet yourself and evaluate your heart condition. If through this time of evaluation, the Holy Spirit brings things to your mind that stand between you and God, then seek His forgiveness (1 John 1:9). It is hard to ask God to fill the cup of your life with His refreshing water when the cup may be a dirty vessel. Take the next fifteen minutes and divide it up into three five-minute sessions. For the first five minutes, read Psalms 27:4 and 63:6 and meditate on God alone. You can close your eyes if you want but certainly close out all distractions around you to center on God. Next, read Joshua 1:8 and Psalm 1:2 and meditate on the Word of God. Finally, read Psalms 143:5 and 145:5 and meditate on His works.

Recently I have had several ministry opportunities that required me to travel. These opportunities took me on the Dan Ryan Expressway in Chicago, the snarled traffic of Seattle, the incredible movement of cars in Phoenix and the sea of faces and elbows in Quito, Ecuador. I remarked to my wife just the other day that the best place to be is at home on our property in the foothills of the Cascade Mountains. It is at this spot—where I can hear the babble of the creek running near our back porch and smell the pure air of the Oregon forest—that I have silence. This particular place I call home is my "sweet spot" of silence.

Not everyone can have the same kind of quiet spots. Some might take a walk in their favorite park or retire to a room in their home and close the door for privacy. Jesus made it a practice to get away from people "to a lonely place" and pray. The point is, we all need to find a spot that provides as much quiet as possible so that we can be still before God.

Do you have your "sweet spot" of silence picked out? Do you go there to hear the voice of God? Quiet. Do you hear it? God is speaking.

STUDY

To study is to acquire knowledge. Bible study is all about reading, interpreting and applying what is read to a one's life. If you desire to be a leader you must read and apply yourself to study. According to Adele Calhoun, the desire of every Christian should be "…to know what the Bible says and how it intersects with my life."[27] Jan Johnson adds, "The purpose of studying the Bible is to get it. We examine the text carefully to comprehend what the Holy Spirit is communicating through the words on the printed page."[28]

As Christians, we must put the CSD of study into active practice. It takes strong and dedicated commitment for reading the Scripture. In doing so, we are making every effort to improve our hearts and minds as believers (Ps. 139:23; Phil. 4:7; 2 Tim. 2:15). We can then hold true to the words of Scripture, continuing in sound doctrine and able to explain the truths of Scripture to others (2 Tim. 2:2). We see that the principles revealed in Scripture are applicable to all of God's people at all times.

Jan Johnson shares that study of the Bible "…is an excellent way of setting oneself up for meditation, because through it you come to understand the main point of the Scripture."[29]

Understanding God's Word is a matter of life and death. In First Corinthians 2:10-16, the description of a spiritual man is found by way of contrast with the natural man. One of the biggest distinctions between the two is that the spiritual man appraises all things, having the mind of Christ. The natural man "…is not even equipped to examine the evidence, let alone pass judgment on a spiritual man."[30] The natural man is temporal, imperfect and weak, while the spiritual man is eternal, perfect and powerful. C. K. Barrett states that the spiritual man is "…not only inspired to understand what he sees; he is also furnished with a moral standard by which all things may be measured."[31] As spiritual men and women, Christians have the great privilege to study and know that God is helping them in their understanding.

When the Bible is studied it becomes real in our lives. It is through this discipline that one practices listening to God, and what better voice to hear! Bible study is a comfort and a true friend for maturing Christians.

WORSHIP

The practices of praying and listening to God lead to worship. This spiritual discipline is about one's response to God. When we worship, we offer honor and praise to God as our response for who He is and all that He has done for us. Such responsiveness brings intimacy with our relational God. It also brings joy to Him as our Creator (Ps. 19:1-4; 33:5-6; 96).

This is because, as Calhoun says, "Human beings were made for worship."[32] Such a divinely built-in purpose can make the life of the Christian one of ceaseless worship. After all, the more people focus on God, the more understanding and appreciation is placed in His worthiness. In this way, Christians can declare God's worth when they worship. Continually.

It has been said, "Worship, rightly understood, begins with the doctrine of the Trinity and the doctrine of image...worship is not merely an aspect of our being, but the essence of our being as God's image bearers."[33]

In his book on worship, Robert Webber states,

"Biblical worship is rooted in an event that is to be lived, not proven."[34] He goes on to declare, "The purpose of worship is not to prove Christ it celebrates, but to bring the worshiper so in tune with God's reconciliation through Christ that His death and resurrection become a lived experience."[35]

In the life of the believer, the "well of worship" needs to run deep. A study in connection to worship bears this out. When the worship well is reduced or empty, the void will usually be filled by idolatry. For many, the source of spiritual trouble is that we love ourselves with a blind love that leads to idolatry.[36] For most Americans (sadly, this includes Christians), there is a strong desire to gratify self. This is done through vacations, spending money, recreation and hobbies, among other things. These activities alone are not the problem, but their abuse is. It is not uncommon for individuals and families to live beyond their monetary income. In doing so, individuals are slaves to debt as the void of worship is filled with the idolatry of things and self. Our national government leads its citizens as examples of this. G. K. Beale states,

> We have seen in Romans 1 that a malfunction in one's relationship to God (e.g., idolatry) brings the corresponding punishment of a malfunction in one's relationship with other humans. But I have also proposed that to some extent Paul's thought appears to include the concept that people become like idols that they venerate, spiritually 'empty.' That this is, in fact, also in mind of Romans 1 is evident further from

the antithetical parallel in Romans 12:1-2. Just as Paul starts the first part of the book with perverted worship, he starts the last part of the book with proper worship acceptable to God. That Paul intends to present Romans 12:1-2 as the antithesis to Romans 1:18-28 is apparent from the use of the terms used oppositely or the use of actual antonyms.[37]

The CSD of worship is essential to a healthy church. Commenting on the gospel understanding of worship and the church, Bryan Chapell writes,

> The order of worship (another way of describing the liturgy) conveys an understanding of the gospel. Whether one intends it or not, our worship patterns always communicate something. Even if one simply goes along with what is either historically accepted or currently preferred, an understanding of the gospel inevitably unfolds. If a leader sets aside time for Confession of Sin (whether by prayer, or by song, or by Scripture reading), then something about the gospel gets communicated. If there is no Confession in the course of service, then something else is communicated – even though the message conveyed may not have been intended.[38]

Psalm 100, a favorite among Christians young and old, describes the greatness and goodness of God. Within its verses is found the simple reason for worship. Christians must worship because they are His people and He is their God.

chapter five

Effective Leadership Marks

EADERSHIP IN ITS MOST BASIC STATE IS HAVING influence over someone. When there are two individuals, one will influence the other and be the leader in that circumstance or situation. Leadership is both upfront and behind the scenes; it is public and private. Jewel Longenecker shares, "...leadership in some measure is about giving people a path to go down. Leaders walk a path; their example creates a path for people to follow."[1] Most people find themselves in a position of leadership, whether as a coach, a teacher or a classmate.

Our seventh grade daughter told her mother and me a story from school about playing the game of "spoons" with her girlfriends. She explained how the game is played and how people can be loud and aggressive along with other antics. My wife made the comment that it didn't sound like a very ladylike game. I asked where the boys were while the girls were playing "spoons." They were playing chess very quietly in the library, she informed us. It almost seemed like role reversal to me that middle school boys would be playing the cerebral game of chess in the library instead of pulling pranks or being loud. The girls, however, were the ones being loud and aggressive instead of thoughtful and quiet. These two groups containing all the boys and all the girls were engaged in two very different activities. When I asked about the leaders of each group, I found that both had gathered friends around an activity he or she personally enjoyed. The boys followed their leader in contemplating a chess board while the girls dove for spoons. This shows us that people have a distinct tendency to follow leadership at any age for reasons significant or otherwise.

One of the most important questions about leadership is, what does the Bible have to say about it? There are a lot of ideas coming out about leadership these days. Cultural ideas about leadership are often contradictory to biblical ones. When contrasting the two, John MacArthur points out, "Much of the world's 'leadership' is nothing but manipulation of people by threats and rewards."[2] Considering the role of the pastor as a spiritual leader, Glenn Daman states,

> The biblical model of the pastor is not, therefore, that of an organizational CEO who effectively runs the organization by setting the vision for the church and guiding the church to growth and organizational health and prosperity. Rather, the biblical model is that of a shep-

herd who provides nourishment and care for the flock.[3]

When thinking of leadership, it is easy to be drawn to First Thessalonians 2:1-12. In this passage three biblical ideas of leadership are at work. The first principle, found in verse eight, is that leaders must impart their lives. Culture is continually encouraging leaders to impress with words, to convey charisma and to refine public persona. But MacArthur states, "…true spiritual leadership is all about character, not style."[4] The biblical passage under consideration expresses that with more than words, Christ's servants imparted their lives. James Kouzes and Barry Posner write about servant leadership:

> Similarly, when leaders affirm the shared values of an organization, they are promising that these values will be kept consistently. The leaders are also saying implicitly that they will be the first to live up to these promises. The ultimate test of a leader's credibility is whether they do what they say. In the doing is where leaders prove to others that they are truly serious about quality or respect or innovation or diversity or whatever the stated value.[5]

When Paul, Timothy and Silas arrived in Thessalonica, they invited people to believe the good news about Jesus and backed up the message with their lives. Verse nine describes their labor and hardship as they worked for their money. In verse ten they were examples of blameless conduct to those living in

Thessalonica. From the outset, Paul declared in verse one that their visit to Thessalonica was not a failure. This statement is a reference to productivity and that there is some substance behind their words. Jesus also modeled this concept. Jesus spoke with very impressive words and could have left it at that, but He came as a man among men. By doing this He imparted His life as a blameless and hard-working man on earth.

The second principle from this passage has to do with power. Paul empowered Thessalonian believers in verse twelve. He reminded them of God's involvement in his life and theirs, encouraging them to live lives worthy of Him. The result of this encouragement was that believers discovered and carried out what God wanted them to do. Today's culture pushes the leader to wield his or her own power, to assert authority and tell people what to do. However, Paul's model was to point people to God for direction.

The third principle in this passage is that the biblical leader must bear pain. This principle is found in First Thessalonians 2:2 and instructs biblical leaders to follow Paul's example to bear pain on behalf of those they influence. This is a striking picture of a shepherd who would sacrifice personal well being on behalf of the sheep. Jesus Christ modeled this dearly by suffering pain and death on the cross for the redemption of mankind.

On the other hand, cultural examples of leadership encourage the enjoyment of privileges. Today's leaders claim entitlements. Therefore it is no wonder that leadership scandals are commonplace in our culture. In many ways leaders have not always held high standards of excellence. As Craig Perrin says,

Effective Leadership Marks

Effective leaders assess their motives, beliefs, attitudes and actions, asking 'How can I ensure my blind spots don't cause poor decisions?' Leaders must take responsibility for their mistakes, seek knowledge to make sense of the big picture, examine what role they play in the challenges they face, treat failure as a chance to learn and grow, reflect on their performance, consider opinions that differ from their own, and speak frankly with others to learn from them and build trust.[6]

Among the various authors, several definitions of leadership can be found. Ken Blanchard and Phil Hodges believe, "Anytime you seek to influence the thinking, behavior, or development of people toward accomplishing a goal in their personal or professional lives, you are taking on the role of a leader."[7] David Hocking says the secret of good leadership is inspiring others to follow your example.[8] In his definition, he emphasizes that a real leader goes before those whom he leads, but not so far ahead of them that he becomes permanently separated from them. He may be able to proceed faster, but if he does this on a consistent basis, he ceases to be a leader. Robert Spitzer states:

What defines a good leader is his or her vision of the common good. So long as a leader 1) yearns for the good of a community (more than self-interest and special interest), 2) has a vision of what the common good would look like, 3) has the prudence to actualize that vision through the diverse groups and 4) has the courage to achieve it with justice, that leader will improve the environment over which he or she has been given authority.[9]

Hudson Armerding shared, "The mark of a Christian leader is a meekness that is bold and decisive in standing for God's Word and God's reputation."[10] This underscores the obvious necessity of a sense of direction if one is to be the leader. Leadership involves both purpose and planning. A leader must be both strategist and tactician. He must have his ultimate goals in mind and also the methods by which he is to reach those goals. He must know where he is going, or he will not know when he gets there. He must know what paths he is going to follow to get there, or he may lose his way. Armerding further stated, "A leader has both natural and supernatural gifts. He is prepared by God for just the right moment to assume his leadership role…. The leader's responsibility is to be available, teachable, and responsible in fulfilling the assignment God gives."[11] The Bible states that the Israelites in Egypt were not to go the direct way to Canaan through the land of the Philistines (Ex. 13:17). They needed the schooling of the Wilderness. But there may have been another reason, not mentioned. The road to Sinai and the region of Sinai were familiar to the leader Moses. He knew the way. A leader understands the way to go.

In his definition, J. Grant Howard said, "Leadership is working with and through individuals and groups to discover and accomplish biblical goals."[12] This definition indicates that the leader must provide motivation if he is going to be successful in his leadership. It is easier to sit still than it is to march; it requires less effort to be a spectator than to be a participant. The leader must motivate those standing on the sidelines to fall into step behind him and those sitting on the bench to get on the playing field. Inspiration must overcome inertia. Irresistible force must unsettle the object thought to be immovable. Andy Stanley writes about the courage to lead and to inspire change as a leadership duty: "Leaders are not always the first to see the need for change, but they are the first to act. And once they move away from the pack, they are positioned to lead."[13]

But instead of multiplying definitions, our attention should turn to a great Christian leader. Essential leadership marks helped make this man a leader whose influence and inspiration have meant so much to the church. The apostle Paul is a true example of the Christ-like leader.

Paul is not the only leader who could be selected out of the Bible. The Bible is filled with teaching about great leaders. The history of the Bible is the history of true heroes. But there is hardly a leader whose influence on the church has been quite as profound as Paul's on the church. One could use a huge mural to paint his life story. The Bible begins by telling about Saul of Tarsus. His conversion was dramatic, and Scripture goes on to tell of Paul the apostle, missionary, prisoner, preacher and writer. Concerning the life of Paul, James Stalker writes, "If Christianity showed its strength in making so complete a conquest of Paul, it showed its worth no less in the kind of man it made him when he had given himself up to its influence."[14]

Even the enemies of truth have been so impressed with his leadership that they say he took the simple teachings of Jesus and turned them into a theology which transformed the church into something it would not otherwise have been.[15]

It was Paul who, under the guidance of his Lord, helped to rescue the Christian faith from circling back into the stream of Judaism and ending up as another Jewish sect and a Dead Sea kind of religion.[16] To say that he alone was responsible is incorrect. The other apostles were not really opposed to him, and they were among countless other Christians who helped him. The Holy Spirit working through Paul and others is the answer. The leadership qualities of Paul were nothing less than a work of God. It is clear that God chose to use Paul as His man for this task. Gene Getz states, "The goal Jesus Christ has for the church, wrote Paul, is to produce 'a mature' body of believers that 'walk worthy' of Christ's calling and measure up to His stature."[17]

The new life in Christ could not be kept in the old channels. New wine could not be put in old wine skins. We cannot deny that it was Paul's leadership, more than any other, which cut the new channel for a movement that would bless the world. He was the trailblazer for the first century church.

Moyer Hubbard comments on Paul's strength and character,

Although not stated explicitly until 2 Cor. 12, this idea of strength cloaked in weakness lies behind Paul's presentation of himself as a conquered foe being led to his death while simultaneously spreading the knowledge of Christ (2

Cor. 2:14-16), or as an earthen vessel concealing great treasure (4:7), as one who is wasting away outwardly but being renewed inwardly (4:16-17), or as one who has nothing yet possesses everything (6:10). Paul is engaged in a long and difficult struggle with the Corinthians over their value system and their superficial evaluation of him, his ministry, and his preaching, and he crystallizes this censure in a paradox of profound magnitude: weakness is strength.[18]

Paul's life cannot be examined in detail here, and the brief summaries that follow cannot do justice to the depth of teaching each mark of his effective leadership could contain. Perhaps your appetite will be whetted to examine them more closely. The following section develops eight characteristics from Paul's life that serve as marks of effective leadership. The disciplines listed and defined in the following chart are in alphabetical order and not necessarily in order of importance.

Effective Leadership Mark Definitions	
Enthusiasm	The lively interest in a particular subject or activity.
Faith	Our belief in Jesus Christ to accomplish the matter.
Hope	Our belief that matters of Christian faith are yet to be.

Humility	Having an accurate and modest opinion of oneself.
Integrity	The outward demonstration of inward belief.
Knowledge	Ability to grasp the inner nature of a situation and see beyond the superficial.
Love	Brotherly affection displayed from one individual to another.
Vision	Our ability to look forward.

ENTHUSIASM

When a leader has a lively interest in a particular subject or activity, people naturally show interest and desire to know more. One of the leaders in the church I pastor is an avid duck hunter. He is enthusiastic about hunting ducks. When he speaks of this enjoyment in his life, it inspires even those who don't hunt, like myself, to get excited.

Enthusiasm is contagious and passionate. Spitzer states, "Excitement toward goal, plus humility, equals inspired leadership toward common cause."[19] Long ago I observed that any successful leader has a spirit of optimism. The pessimist never makes it. Enthusiasm does not have to be boisterous since quieter, controlled enthusiasm is more lasting.

Effective Leadership Marks

Defeatism is also contagious. It can spread like a plague. Organizations seek stability or the status quo to prevent change, and the leader must challenge this.[20] Defeatism has caused many to abandon dreams and cripple their leadership. Thomas Edison invented the light bulb, but earlier in life was kicked out of school. Michael Jordan has become a household name and sports icon, he has been designated by many as the greatest basketball player ever, yet he was cut from the varsity basketball team during his sophomore year of high school. Walt Disney brought joy to millions of people through the medium of animated films, but only after being fired from a newspaper job and being told he had no cartoonist ability. Abraham Lincoln is remembered as one of the greatest presidents of the United States of America, yet he suffered defeat in eight elections and a nervous breakdown before finally taking the nation's highest office. Defeatism and status quo can cripple a movement. It can thwart a worthy project and derail a life headed for divine purpose. There ought to be some kind of isolation ward in the church for those who become affected by it!

Enthusiasm is demonstrated by displaying a positive attitude, smiling, good body language, appropriate speech for the occasion and tasteful clothing. These are some of the many examples that indicate you are an enthusiastic person. Enthusiasm is both personal and others-oriented. A positive presentation of self toward others demonstrates enthusiasm. Conversely, a negative presentation of self demonstrates defeatism.

The apostle Paul was an enthusiast. He had learned

in whatever state he found himself not only to be content, not only to accept his circumstances, but to rejoice while in them (Phil. 4:4). Throughout his life, this suffering saint kept shouting the word, "Rejoice!" He was more than stoic; he was genuinely Christian. He had caught the spirit of his Master who called back over His shoulder on the way to the cross, "In this world you will have trouble. But take heart! I have overcome the world" (John 16:33).

With abundant zeal, boundless enthusiasm and unquenchable faith, the apostle Paul blazed a trail across his world winning converts, starting new churches, encouraging older churches, training Christian leaders and injecting energy and life into the whole Christian movement.

FAITH

Closely linked to enthusiasm is faith. In fact, enthusiasm and vision are the outgrowths of a genuine faith. Faith is the foundation; enthusiasm and vision are part of the superstructure. Because the apostle Paul really believed, he had vision. Because his faith in Christ was so constant and complete, he had enthusiasm. The faith of Paul is described by Dallas Willard: "The faith by which Jesus Christ lived, his faith in God and His kingdom, is expressed in the gospel that He preached. That gospel is the good news that the kingdom rule of God is available to humankind here and now."[21]

It is important to note that if Paul had not become a Christian, he probably would still have been a leader. He was obviously crippled by a growing uncertainty about his prejudices and beliefs. The death of Stephen and the lives of Christians were making their impact. But even so, he led the opposition against Christ.

All of this changed the day of the Damascus Road experience. From that day on, his faith in the risen Christ more than perhaps any other single factor made him the world leader he became. In Philippians 4:13 we read that, "I can do everything through him who gives me strength." Concerning Paul's former way of life, Barrett states, "Faith is not essentially a matter of turning away from a bad way of life; it is equally, and at a deeper level, a turning away from a good life in which one depends on one's own achievement, one's own works done in obedience to the moral law."[22] Again to the church at Philippi, Paul assured, "And my God will meet your needs according to his riches in Christ Jesus" (Phil. 4:19). To the church at Corinth he declared, "God is able to make all grace abound to you, so that in all things at all times, having all that you need, you will abound in every good work" (2 Cor. 9:8). These verses show how Paul's perspective changed. Saul had become Paul through the transformation of his soul, and his faith was strengthened.

In order for faith to be operative in Christian experience, someone must give His Word; He must make a promise. This principle is clearly stated as follows: "Consequently, faith comes from hearing the message, and the message is heard through the Word of Christ" (Rom. 10:17). Faith is the basis of hope, and the Word of God is the basis of the Christian's faith. Unbelievers may want to know what reason

Christians have for believing what they believe and how they know those beliefs are true. In other words, what is the basis of their faith? There can only be one answer. The faith of the Christian rests in the promises of Jesus Christ as found in Scripture. Faith begins in the Word. There must be a report of a promise to be believed, and there must be a hearing. Therefore if all men are to have the opportunity to believe, then the prerequisite must be the proclamation of the good news promised by God. Without the Word (the promise), there could be no ground for faith.

But suppose a man is without faith? Paul anticipates just such a question: "What if some did not have faith? Will their lack of faith nullify God's faithfulness?" (Rom. 3:3). It is as though he were asking, "What if some were without faith? Does the absence of faith render God unfaithful?" Answering first the second part of the question, God is not unfaithful or else He would cease to be God. Paul states very clearly in First Corinthians 1:9, "God...is faithful." The Scriptures designate Him as the "faithful God, keeping his covenant of love..." (Deut. 7:9); the "... faithful Creator..." (1 Pet. 4:19), "...faithful and just and will forgive us our sins" (1 John 1:9); "...God...is faithful; He will not let you be tempted beyond what you can bear..."(1 Cor. 10:13).

Where there is no faith, one has either not heard or else has not yielded one's heart to the Lord. Faith is the readiness to let God be whom He means to be and to thank Him for being God. Paul stated in Romans 3:4, "Let God be true, and every man a liar." He continued to proclaim, "...faith comes from hearing the message, and the message is heard through the word of

Christ" (Rom. 10:17). At this point the warning must be sounded so that we hear the words of God rather than the words of man. Paul warns against "using wise and persuasive words…so that your faith might not rest on men's wisdom, but on God's power" (1 Cor. 2:4-5). Words have a tremendous power of persuasion, so we must be on guard at all times against those who speak persuasive words that are not God's. Peter described false teachers in Second Peter 2:18, "They mouth empty, boastful words…," and Jude 16 stated, "They boast about themselves and flatter others for their own advantage."

The one who knows that supplies are inexhaustible, resources are adequate and living supplies will not be cut off will keep moving. And the one who keeps moving will be a leader among others.

What a need there is today for this fruit of the Spirit called faith! To those outside of the church, Christians seem concerned about what they believe. However, they need to manifest just as much concern about whether they believe. Christians must be characterized by an invincible, unconquerable faith that brings an answer from God so they can silence the arguments of the critics.

If someone needs more faith, he or she must by all means get it. The apostles cried out for it: "Lord, increase our faith" (Luke 17:5). And then they listened to Jesus's teaching. There is no shortcut aside from spending time with God.

HOPE

Hope is the expectation of good things in the

future.[23] The apostle Paul stated, "...hope does not disappoint us, because God has poured out his love into our hearts by the Holy Spirit, whom he has given us" (Rom. 5:5). It is closely connected to the biblical concept of faith. Biblical hope finds its basis in the promises of God contained in the Bible. Conversely, those who do not believe in God and His promises resort to reasoning found outside the Bible. David Hansen writes, "Some can only hope for things that directly benefit themselves."[24] Paul wrote to the church at Ephesus to remind the believers to "remember that at that time you were separate from Christ, excluded from citizenship in Israel and foreigners to the covenants of promise, without hope and without God in the world" (Eph. 2:12). Believers in Jesus Christ have hope by faith regarding the matters that are yet to be, not in themselves or circumstances. For Paul, the source of all hope is in God (Rom. 15:13).

Faith and hope are closely linked. The writer of Hebrews shared, "Now faith is being sure of what we hope for and certain of what we do not see" (Heb. 11:1). Thomas Schreiner shares, "One of the marks of authentic faith is perseverance, and faith perseveres because it is sustained by hope."[25] This hope that Paul preached rested squarely on God's calling and upon His promises (Rom. 4:17-21). For Paul there was only one hope (Eph. 4:4). That hope was "...vital to the Christian experience, since both faith in Christ and love for other believers are grounded in hope...."[26] The apostle Paul wrote to the church at Rome, "For everything that was written in the past was written to teach us, so that through endurance and the encouragement of the Scriptures we might have hope" (Rom.

15:4). The hope Paul had in Christ made him a dedicated and godly leader.

HUMILITY

Humility can be described as having an accurate and modest opinion of oneself. Paul did not plan to become a leader of men and churches to the extent that he was, let alone start a worldwide movement. His vision, enthusiasm, faith, knowledge – and the sovereign Holy Spirit – thrust him into that position.

Once there, his humility made him a man easy to follow. The man who said he was "…less than the least of all God's people" (Eph. 3:8) and when bidding farewell to the elders of Ephesus said he had "…served the Lord with great humility and with tears" (Acts 20:19), secured a faithful, loyal following wherever he went.

This quality is basic to all ELMs. Humility towards men is the only sufficient proof that humility before God is real. This is significant because the events of daily life are the tests of eternity. Alan Andrews shares, "Humility is the first and most important particle in a community of grace, because more than any other, humility is both the way into and the means for living in the community."[27]

Humility is simply the disposition which prepares the souls living on trust. Its possessors trust God and others. Spitzer says,

> Humility shares greatness generously by allowing others back in the achievement of great vision, to recognize and appreciate people for their contribution to this collective enterprise,

and to allow people to feel their true importance and dignity in light of their invaluable
contribution.[28]

The blessings of the highest Christian life are often
like objects displayed in a store window – one can see
them clearly, yet cannot reach them. If told to stretch
out his hand and take what he wanted, a man answers,
I cannot touch because of the thick plate of glass in
between. What is it that hinders? Nothing but pride!
Spitzer goes on to share that humility "…is the most
important means of achieving higher viewpoints, and
is therefore an absolute prerequisite to inspired leadership."[29] Humility is the beauty of holiness.

If only Christians, with God's help by some spiritual chemistry of the soul, could extract the pride that
plagues today's pulpits and the conceit that cripples
their leadership! Their ranks must be filled by person-
nel who will humbly follow, and leadership is needed
that will humbly lead. Every display of authority used
wrongly lessens authority, while evidence of genuine
humility attracts a following.

INTEGRITY

I am amazed with the technology that provides
a traveler with pinpoint directions. Smart phones
and certain models of automobiles come with global
positioning systems (GPS) as standard accessories.
So many times I have been traveling and found this
feature to be beneficial to arriving at a correct destination! I fear that many Christian leaders have lost
their internal GPS. For many, the internal signals of

the heart are not processing together with the Spirit of God. In essence, integrity – the outward demonstration of inward belief – has been lost. An individual cannot mean what they say if they have lost the connection to their heart and soul. Someone has said, "If we do not stand for something, we will fall for everything." What has happened to personal integrity among believers? Firm principles to live by, professional standards, biblical ethics of morality and other foundational virtues among Christians have been corrupted by the world system we live in. Is it any wonder that diluted Christian leadership is linked to scandal? Lives are not right; attitudes are not right; actions are not right.

What people believe determines how they behave, and both determine what they become. According to John 8:31-32, if Christians believe truth, it will set them free. If they believe lies, they will gradually become like a lie as integrity is lost. The apostle Paul sought to live above reproach with high ideals and character as he exemplified this: "So I strive always to keep my conscience clear before God and man" (Acts 24:16). His striving paid off. He made mistakes, and for these he could be criticized. He may have been impatient and intolerant of John Mark at Perga and Peter at Antioch, but he had his reasons. These incidents only underscore his integrity. The cause of Christ was enhanced by his integrity.

Leadership has to be earned; it can never be conferred. Every time a leader accepts a new position, he or she must both wait and work to establish leadership with those who are to follow. A reputation for successful leadership elsewhere does not automatically qualify someone for leadership in a new position. Integrity must be demonstrated, and by integrity the corollaries of dependability, honesty, purity and consistency are exemplified.

KNOWLEDGE

I asked a colleague what was considered the chief characteristic of leadership. The response was immediate, "Knowledge: a leader must know the direction he is going to take!"

Knowledge supposes facts (truths) about people or things. To know something or someone is to have understanding. To say that you know a person is to have some understanding about their character. To state that you know the game of basketball supposes that you understand the concept of the game, as well as rules and facts about it.

Pursuing only knowledge can be dangerous. Solomon declared, "Then I applied myself to the understanding of wisdom. And also of madness and folly, but I learned that this, too, is a chasing after wind. For with much wisdom comes much sorrow; the more knowledge, the more grief" (Eccl. 1:17-18). The knowledge of this world opposes the truth of God (1 Tim. 6:20-21).

When the Bible describes knowledge, it uses God as the standard (Rom. 11:33). True knowledge must begin with God (Prov. 1:7) for He has made it known. Jesus described knowledge in the context of a personal relationship between the believer and the Savior of the world, "If you hold to my teaching, you are really my disciples. Then you will know the truth, and the truth will set you free" (John 8:31-32). Peter proclaimed, "For this very reason, make every effort to add to your faith goodness; and to goodness, knowledge" (2 Pet. 1:5).

We can summarize Paul's pre-conversion training in one phrase: he was an educated man (Acts 22:3). The whole course of Paul's life after his conversion cannot be traced. There are two main periods in his Christian life which are obscure – one shortly after he became a Christian and the other near the end of his career. All that is known is that he went to Arabia some time after his meeting with Christ. Paul asked who Jesus was in Acts 9:5, and the Lord answered by telling him what to do in Acts 9:6. He may have spent three years in Arabia to find out. This training period was perhaps a time of unlearning the worldly knowledge he had and a fresh learning of godliness. Not surprisingly, Paul told Timothy, "Do not be hasty in the laying on of hands…"(1 Tim. 5:22). Perhaps Paul learned that time itself was another teacher of knowledge as future leaders of the church are developed. In other words, do not thrust a man into leadership before he is ready. Paul practiced what he preached. His life and ministry had a sense of direction and purpose.

The leader must also have a perceptiveness which often comes through training. This individual must be able to grasp the inner nature of a situation, to see behind the superficial. Otherwise the leader will make decisions on the basis of a surface observation. One reason the phrase, "Barnabas and Saul," was altered to read, "Paul and Barnabas," is that Paul saw the course, core and consequences of a given situation. Part of this perceptiveness he got in the desert of Arabia.

Some characteristics of leadership are difficult to attain. They seem to be inborn. Some are simply born to be leaders. But knowledge is a characteristic within the reach of every normal, intelligent Christian worker. In the field of Christian leadership today there is an abundance of reliable resources and opportunities for learning not available to previous generations. It is incumbent on the people of the Church to utilize these resources.

LOVE

The one word to which all of Scripture and the events of earthly history are nailed is love. To understand love is to understand God. Love appears in the Scriptures as one of the supreme attributes of God.[30] One of the highest forms of this attribute of God in mankind seeks the welfare of others.[31] Jesus stated, "'Love the Lord your God with all your heart and with all your soul and with all your mind.' This is the first and greatest commandment. And the second is like it. 'Love your neighbor as yourself'" (Matt. 22:37-40). Jesus does not tiptoe around the issue of pride and love of self in His command. Instead, he goes right to the root of sin. In the first command, the focus is on God and how our happiness must reside completely in Him. The second command opens the door of joy to the whole world. Believers must love all people!

Frank Magill commented on love from a manuscript written in the year 640 by Saint Maximus the Confessor stating, "Love for others is a key element in the contemplative life; it acts as a sort of measure for one's purity. The concept of obedience finds its most important expression in love."[32] We must love all people "... equally – with money ... and service – regardless of whether they are just or unjust, just as God loves all equally."[33]

Concerning pastoral theology and the implications of a pastor's love for the church, David Fisher writes:

> I realized the powerful implications. If the pastor is like a parent, the church is a family. It is a place to grow. It is where people love you simply because you belong to them. There you are always welcome and are cared for and kept safe from harm. Family love is foundational and is so deep in us that it defies description. But we sure do know it when we have it! If anything is certain on this fallen planet filled with uncertainties and broken promises, it is that my mother and father love me.[34]

Love was revealed at the cross for mankind (John 3:16) and was displayed through the death of Christ for all mankind (Rom. 5:8). Jesus was made the sin offering for the world (2 Cor. 5:21).

For Paul, the command to love our neighbor is the "fulfillment of the law" (Rom. 13:8-10). His love was dependent on his relationship with God (Rom. 8:3-4). For the Christian leader, to love God is to love people.

VISION

It is possible to idealize Paul unduly. But it is quite safe to say, however, that Paul would have been a leader regardless of the goals he might have chosen. This is evident by his rapid rise to leadership in the opposition to Jesus Christ and His followers (Acts 26:9).

But never would Paul have become such a leader apart from the great vision which came to possess him from his encounter with the risen Christ. Here were objectives that called for the highest, the holiest and the hardest. There was a world to reach; there was a message to preach; there was a truth to teach. Bill Hybels writes about vision: "When God finally brings clarity and certainty of vision in a leader's life, everything changes for the better."[35] That was certainly true in Paul's life.

The geography of Paul's life is thrilling. In Romans 15:19 he declared that his personal ministry had stretched from Jerusalem to Illyricum. The last outpost in Italy was Illyricum. This is why the book of Romans was written. He had gone as far as he could go, and now (Romans 15:23) he was on his way to Rome. But Rome was only a stopover in his proposed itinerary (Rom. 15:24) before he hoped to go to Spain, the western tip of Paul's world. Paul was one of the busiest of the New Testament travelers.

My uncle, a Blackfoot Indian, told me how the young braves were sent out to a secluded spot in the forest for a period of fasting and meditation with the Great Spirit before assuming the responsibilities of adulthood. With blackened face, a young man was to wait until the Great Spirit would reveal to him by dream or vision the course of his life. Occasionally among the tribe there were those who seemed to have no drive or ambition. They were the ones who returned prematurely without waiting until the vision and inspiration came.

A leader must have vision. To be forward-looking is a leadership prerequisite. James Kouzes and Barry Posner write,

> You can have a lasting legacy only if you can imagine a brighter future, and the capacity to imagine exciting future possibilities is the defining competence of leaders. Today's leaders have to be concerned about tomorrow's world and those who will inherit it. They are the custodians of the future, and it's their job to make sure that they leave their organizations in better shape than they found them.[36]

God had a vision and a plan for His creation (Gen. 1-2). He made plans for the salvation of mankind (Eph. 3:10-11). Jesus had a vision and plan for the disciples (Matt. 28:19-20). Through the direction of the Holy Spirit the apostles made plans (Acts 16:6-10). Paul provided vision and plans for the equipping of the Body of Christ, His Church (Eph. 4:11-16). All Christians, but especially leaders, need to have vision for their lives and the church. Someone has said that life is hard, and when poor decisions are made it is harder. Lacking vision and direction in life makes life more difficult than it should be. To have vision shows good thought, responsibility and stewardship. Lacking vision results in confusion, apathy and laziness.

Paul's name might have been found in some footnote of history if he had continued to live in opposition to Christ. But there was something greater in life for him than this. From the greater vision to live Christ and preach Christ, there emerged the greater leader. One of the most important marks of leadership is vision.

chapter six

Theological Support

WHEN CHRISTIANS TALK ABOUT SPIRITUAL growth in their lives, theology plays an important part. The substance and character of a believer can be described in theological terms. Core spiritual disciplines (CSDs) and effective leadership marks (ELMs) can be described theologically as well. The aspects of theology that have direct bearing on these areas are developed in this chapter.

The first is ecclesiology which is the study of the church. The second is pneumatology, the study of the Holy Spirit. The third is sanctification, the process of making a believer holy.

ECCLESIOLOGY

One's understanding of ecclesiology determines a theological direction for an individual. The Body of Christ provides the perfect setting to understand and practice spiritual disciplines.

The answer one gives to "What is the church?" is important. Basic to understanding the answer is the biblical usage of the word that is translated in the English language as "church." This Greek word, *ekklesia,* means an "assembly, meeting or congregation."

In this book, the term "church" refers to all believers in Jesus Christ. Mark Driscoll and Gerry Breshears describe the church in this way:

> The local church is a community of regenerated believers who confess Jesus Christ as Lord. In obedience to Scripture they organize under qualified leadership, gather regularly for preaching and worship, observe the biblical sacraments of baptism and Communion, are unified by the Spirit, are disciplined for holiness, and scatter to fulfill the Great Commandment and the Great Commission as missionaries to the world for God's glory and their joy.[1]

Donald Whitney encourages us to consider the church as members who are personally engaged with one another instead of being separate unto themselves by stating:

> The church is a community in which Christians are to live and experience much of their Christianity. Too many believers isolate themselves from life with the family of God, deceived by the notion that "me and Jesus" are all they need in order to be all that God wants them to become and to savor all He has for them. Such individualization of the faith hurts the church. What too

few see is that anything that hurts the church eventually hurts them as individual Christians.[2]

One's personal actions before the Lord have direct bearing on the church as a whole. Attendance, giving, serving, suffering, membership, to name a few, affect the health of a local assembly. It is quite easy for one to point out the shortcomings of a local church, but I am convinced that if people living in close proximity to a local gospel-preaching church would fully embrace its ministry, then the number of struggling churches would sharply decline. As local churches see individuals become faithful in attendance, and as members function within the church according to Scripture, whole communities could be changed for the good. Special urgency is needed for personal decisions to be made about these matters of personal actions. The time is crucial. We have a great commission to fulfill (Matt. 28:19-20), not to ignore and omit from our lives. For adults with children at home who are struggling with these matters, let me remind you that your children are watching. The next generation of young people growing up into adulthood are staying away from church in historic numbers. The impact of parents' examples and attitudes cannot be ignored.

The church also depends on good leadership. The people of the church will grow no higher than they are challenged to grow by the example of the leadership. The church provides fertile ground for prayer, worship, confession, life together, fasting, study, service and silence to be practiced and observed. My study of the relationship of CSDs and ELMs in nine churches shows sixty-six fields of data that received very strong correlations above .80 and one hundred seven correlations above .50. The church is the benefactor of these very strong correlations of CSDs and ELMs because its leadership provides living examples of how elements of the two areas work together effectively.

PNEUMATOLOGY

The word pneumatology comes from the Greek word *pneuma*, which means "spirit." The psalmist said that the Spirit of God is everywhere (Ps. 139:7). His first work in the life of the believer is when He is given as a mark of inheritance at the time of salvation (Eph. 1:13-14).

To understand the work of the Holy Spirit, it is important see the church as a body. The Holy Spirit forms the church by baptizing all believers into the body of Christ. As such, each believer is necessary and has unique importance. This describes the role of the individual Christian as well as the leader. As part of the body of Christ, each has a specific ministry that God has given him or her to perform. Every member is needed if the body is to function as it should. It is imperative, therefore, that each Christian and leader recognize his or her distinctive place in the body of Christ and the divine provision to exercise his or her unique ministry through the enablement of the Holy Spirit.

The effective practice of spiritual disciplines is a work of the Holy Spirit. The Holy Spirit regenerates and conforms believers to the image of Jesus Christ (Rom. 8:29; Gal. 4:19). It is the Holy Spirit who fills and provides guidance to Christians (Eph. 5:18). The

Holy Spirit gives power to individuals (Acts 1:8). The Holy Spirit of God enables Christians to experience Him and hear His voice through the Spirit (1 Cor. 2:6-16). The Holy Spirit will teach people and remind them to be godly (John 14:26). Those who live the Christian life must be led by the Spirit of God (Rom. 8:12-17) and obey His counsel at every opportunity. Christians must not gratify the desires of the sinful nature because the Spirit and the sinful nature are in conflict with one another (Gal. 5:16-18). The Holy Spirit helps believers encounter God and live fuller lives in Christ by practicing CSDs daily.

The Holy Spirit works through CSDs to reveal areas of weakness and need and then provide remedy. When one practices the CSD of study, it is promised that his or her way will be kept pure (Ps. 119:9-11). When silence is practiced, the voice of God can be heard and wonderful benefits come (Matt. 6:33). The leader dealing with scandal can find forgiveness by confession and become a person of integrity by practicing silence (reflected by the very strong correlation which will be viewed later in chapter seven).

SANCTIFICATION

Sanctification, the process of becoming holy, begins at the time of salvation. It involves the act of God through the Holy Spirit to bring change in the believer's life (1 Thess. 5:23; Gal. 5:22-23). "Continue to workout your salvation with fear and trembling, for it is God who works in you to will and to act according to his good purpose" wrote Paul in Philippians 2:13-14. This outworking of the believer's life describes the process of sanctification. Thomas Schreiner elaborates,

> For Paul, then, sanctification usually refers to the definitive work by which God has set apart believers in the realm of the holy in Christ Jesus. The eschatological work is accomplished at conversion, so that believers can be said to be holy or sanctified in God's presence. Still, Paul recognizes the need for growth in holiness and that transformation is a process (2 Cor. 3:18), since complete sanctification and holiness will not be granted until Christ returns. Believers are already holy in Christ, and yet the fullness of that holiness will not be theirs until the day of redemption.[3]

Sanctification is a vital relationship between God and His people. Richard Holland notes, "Every part of a Christian's holiness – past, present, and future – comes from God Himself and His power. The commands to be holy are given to individuals who will give a personal account to God.[4]

Peter described believers as chosen, holy and a people belonging to God (1 Peter 2:9). Leaders are called to present themselves holy to God (Rom. 12:1-2). The writer of Hebrews declared, "Make every effort to … be holy" (Heb. 12:14). For the pastor, then, Holland advises,

> Instruction about sanctification, accountability to the process of sanctification, and exemplifying personal sanctification should be among

the highest priorities for a pastor. Sanctification is the dimension of salvation that consumes the whole of the believer's life…. Surprisingly, the necessity of sanctification is often absent. Yet, sanctification is an essential component of the gospel of Jesus Christ and occupies the largest concern of a Christian's life on earth.[5]

"So be holy in all you do" is a clear command found in First Peter 1:15. The practice of CSDs are fitting examples of holy living which believers can apply. As Andrew Murray pointed out, "The knowledge of the greatness and the glory of Jesus is the secret of a strong and holy life."[6]

What do CSDs have to do with ELMs? What does helping leaders understand the correlations of spiritual disciplines have to do with the development and act of leadership? Part Three of this book suggests answers from leadership in established churches. It also raises warning flags and questions.

"Love is the greatest thing that God can give us, for himself is love; and it is the greatest thing we can give to God.... It is the work of all other graces, without any instrument but its own immediate virtue."

Jeremy Taylor, Rules and Exercises of Holy Living (London: Bell and Daldy Fleet Street, 1857), 254.

"The saints in heaven shall enjoy God and the Lamb, by sight, and that is the most perfect manner."

Thomas Boston, Human Nature in its Fourfold State (Philadelphia: Towar and J. and D. M. Hogan, 1830), 355.

part three

Moving Ahead

"Eloquence and learning are highly necessary; but, if found alone, they never give the preacher the power of persuasion."

John Smith, *Lectures on the Nature and End of the Sacred Office* (Baltimore: A. Neal, 1810), 138.

"Making a difference in the lives of others is so important. One American Indian tribe has an old saying that goes, 'When you were born you cried and the world rejoiced. Live your life in such a way that when you die the world cries and you rejoice.'"

James C. Hunter, *Servant* (New York: Crown Business, 1998), 176.

chapter seven

Evaluating the Data

THIS SHOULD NOT COME AS A SURPRISE: SPIRITUAL
disciplines make a difference in church leadership. In this chapter is a study showing that CSDs and
ELMs are bound together by verified data. But this
study goes deeper than that. Certain disciplines are
linked to certain leadership traits. A church can use
this information as a guide to know which disciplines
can help their leaders develop in areas of leadership
that are lacking. Say vision, for example. What CSDs
show high correlations with that leadership mark? Or
what if the elders lack enthusiasm? What disciplines
may help them gain in that area for the benefit of the
church?

In addition to being a guide, the data provides
warnings for the church. Negative correlations indicate areas that are lacking and suggest ways to solve
the problem. Also, when correlations vary widely
among demographic areas, questions arise.

Applying what the data shows about the relationships between CSDs and ELMs, we can see what's ahead—the prize of transformed leadership.

Correlation of Core Spiritual Disciplines and Effective Leadership Marks According to Demographics

This section identifies correlations in urban, suburban and rural churches that were based on the "Leaders' Questionnaire" (APPENDIX A). This questionnaire was given to nine churches: three urban, three suburban and three rural. The leaders (deacons, elders and pastors) were each given the questionnaire to complete and return. These questionnaires were then tabulated to find the data contained in Tables 1-4 of this chapter.

Tables 1-4 have a total of sixty-four fields of data apiece. Each field represents a correlation which is defined as "…the degree to which two or more attributes or measurements on the same group of elements show a tendency to vary together."[1] These values were obtained by using the Pearson product-moment correlation coefficient.[2] Standard social science data analysis would characterize correlations as follows: 0-.2 very weak, .2-.4 weak, .4-.6 moderate, .6-.8 strong and .8-.10 very strong. Very strong correlations (both positive and negative) are noted in the text for each demographic area as well as the total.

Tables 1-4 show CSDs arranged along the left side of each graph and ELMs arranged across the top of each graph.

Table 1: Correlation of CSDs and ELMs – Urban

URBAN	Vision	Enthusiasm	Humility	Integrity	Knowledge	Faith	Hope	Love
Prayer	0.788	0.988	0.541	-0.063	0.365	0.092	0.365	0.781
Worship	0.349	0.92	0.901	0.468	0.798	0.6	0.798	0.992
Confession	-0.586	0.185	0.86	0.994	0.943	0.998	0.943	0.652
Life Together	0.841	0.97	0.461	-0.155	0.277	0	0.277	0.72
Fasting	-0.488	0.297	0.913	0.976	0.975	0.998	0.975	0.735
Study	0.998	0.72	-0.044	-0.628	-0.24	-0.5	-0.24	0.277
Service	0.946	0.884	0.234	-0.388	0.038	-0.24	0.038	0.532
Silence	-0.391	0.399	0.952	0.947	0.993	0.985	0.993	0.804

URBAN

Core spiritual disciplines reflecting key correlations include prayer, worship, confession, life together, fasting, study, service and silence. Effective leadership marks that are key correlations include vision, enthusiasm, humility, integrity, knowledge, faith, hope and love. The very strongest correlations (.995 and above) link study and vision, confession and faith, and fasting and faith. Negative correlations are not low enough to be considered significant.

SUBURBAN

Core spiritual disciplines that are key correlations include prayer, worship, confession, study, service and silence. Effective leadership marks that are key correlations include vision, enthusiasm, humility, integrity, knowledge, faith, hope and love. The very strongest correlations (.997 and above) pair silence and integrity, study and knowledge, service and knowledge, and study and hope. The three very strong negative correlations are all in the area of fasting: fasting and enthusiasm, fasting and humility, and fasting and love.

Table 2: Correlation of CSDs and ELMs – Suburban

SUB-URBAN	Vision	Enthusiasm	Humility	Integrity	Knowledge	Faith	Hope	Love
Prayer	0.957	0.537	0.662	0.979	0.995	0.887	0.987	0.151
Worship	0.943	0.5	0.628	0.987	0.989	0.866	0.979	0.107
Confession	0.622	0.981	0.94	0.176	0.458	0.755	0.509	0.974
Life Together	-0.366	0.327	0.176	-0.076	-0.539	-0.19	-0.49	0.681
Fasting	-0.606	-0.978	-0.933	-0.157	-0.441	-0.74	-0.49	-0.98
Study	0.991	0.669	0.776	0.933	0.997	0.951	0.999	0.312
Service	0.841	0.58	0.7	0.968	0.998	0.909	0.994	0.202
Silence	0.982	0.286	0.431	0.997	0.929	0.726	0.907	-0.13

Table 3: Correlation of CSDs and ELMs – Rural[3]

Prayer	0.5	0.419	0.885	0.5	0.887	0.777	0.553	0.5
Worship	0.5	0.419	0.885	0.5	0.887	0.777	0.553	0.5
Confession	0.716	0.157	0.726	0.716	0.979	0.577	0.306	0.246
Life Together	0.785	0.052	0.65	0.785	0.995	0.488	0.204	0.142
Fasting	-0.866	0.907	0.463	-0.866	-0.461	0.628	0.833	0.866
Study	0.726	-0.98	-0.656	0.726	0.243	-0.79	-0.94	-0.96
Service	-0.023	0.83	0.997	-0.023	0.518	0.991	0.905	0.877
Silence	-1	0.576	-0.041	-1	-0.842	0.155	0.444	0.5

RURAL

Core spiritual disciplines that are key correlations include service, fasting, life together, confession, worship and prayer. Effective leadership marks that are key correlations include enthusiasm, humility, knowledge, faith, hope and love. The very strongest correlations pair off humility and service, knowledge and confession, knowledge and life together and service and faith. The lowest negative correlations (-.95 and below) link silence and vision, silence and integrity, study and enthusiasm, and study and love.

TOTAL

Core spiritual disciplines that are key correlations for all nine churches include prayer, confession and service. Effective leadership marks that are key correlations include enthusiasm, humility and faith. The very strongest correlations couple prayer and enthusiasm, service and enthusiasm, service and humility, and confession and faith. The range of correlations is smaller in this table (possibly due to the larger sample of all nine churches' responses) so there are no negative correlations.

Table 4: Correlation of CSDs and ELMs – Total

RURAL	Vision	Enthusiasm	Humility	Integrity	Knowledge	Faith	Hope	Love
Prayer	0.689	0.818	0.618	0.3	0.525	0.439	0.414	0.489
Worship	0.557	0.743	0.785	0.427	0.691	0.596	0.553	0.516
Confession	0.437	0.48	0.761	0.699	0.76	0.904	0.62	0.489
Life Together	0.55	0.783	0.728	0.268	0.476	0.587	0.393	0.597
Fasting	0.041	0.023	0.3	0.569	0.511	0.694	0.415	0.067
Study	0.78	0.555	0.299	0.376	0.472	0.151	0.134	0.19
Service	0.655	0.825	0.873	0.347	0.556	0.623	0.781	0.714
Silence	0.457	0.544	0.548	0.6	0.727	0.758	0.707	0.439

What We Can Learn from the Church Settings

Each church setting—urban, suburban and rural—has its own unique combination of positive and negative points based on the strongest correlations. Positive correlations provide helpful tips while negative correlations give warnings.

The urban setting shows the positive combinations of study and vision, confession and faith, and fasting and faith. From this we can learn that leaders who apply themselves to study will be able to understand what God wants for the future. Also, both confession and fasting are vital to faith. Confession may be difficult since those in an urban setting may have a more jaded outlook on life and be more guarded in areas of trust and relationships because of their environment. Fasting also may be difficult, since it is not taught in the church very often and few examples exist of people who practice it. Yet the strength of the correlation shows that a significant number of leaders who fast and confess show strong indication of faith.

The suburban setting shows the positive combinations of silence and integrity, study and knowledge, and study and hope. Integrity comes as a result of silence, possibly due to the inward reflective nature of silence and its effect on behavior. The link in study and knowledge is obvious since one studies to gain knowledge. Service paired with knowledge conveys the whole idea of serving others. As leaders gain knowledge from Scripture about servanthood, they are able to model it in many creative ways. Concerning study and hope, leaders who study God's Word learn to hope for the things Scripture teaches Christians to hope for. One of the apostle Paul's strong teaching points was to know the hope that is in the believer (Col. 1:27). This correlation reflects that hope is truly valued in the suburban setting, and people are seeking hope in every possible area. Whether it is people trying to move toward jobs or move away from cities, the suburban mindset seeks refuge. Leaders are looking for hope in silence, study, worship and prayer (all very strong correlations above .90).

The suburban setting also shows a number of negative correlations, all associated with fasting: fasting and enthusiasm, fasting and love, and fasting and humility. These areas may serve as warnings to incorporate fasting in its true sense—as mourning over sin—more often. For those leaders who did not rate themselves well in enthusiasm, love or humility, did not see fasting as important. But the lack of love and the lack of humility (pride) are sins which call for repentance. Fasting would be an appropriate response.

The rural setting is rich in insightful correlations. Strong correlations include service and humility, confession and knowledge, and life together and knowledge. Serving others brings humility. Service also shows high correlations with faith and hope. Rural leaders show this genuine expression of the Christian life more readily. The strong correlation of confession and knowledge makes sense based on the definitions of the terms. To confess is to agree with God that He is right about a particular matter and the one confessing is wrong. Knowledge conveys the idea that one has the ability to grasp the inner nature of the situation and see beyond the superficial. Rural leaders seem to understand this connection. Life together and knowledge demonstrates that rural leaders see the intrinsic need for gathering together and value it. Face-to-face encounters are important.

Four strong negative correlations are noticeable in the rural setting: Silence is paired with both vision and integrity, study is paired with both enthusiasm and love. This indicates that silence may not be practiced as a spiritual discipline in this setting. It may be easier to find but not necessarily sought. But silence before God is necessary before vision or integrity can germinate. Negative correlations with study relate to a mindset of indifference toward study or the lack of time to devote to it. Coupled with enthusiasm, the correlation may show preference for soberness and a steady outlook. Concerning love (brotherly love), displays of affection toward other Christians may not be appreciated. But these negative areas again can serve as warnings. Silence and study should be encouraged so as to foster vision, integrity, enthusiasm and love.

Churches should build their ministries and programs around the strong points of their leadership. This study suggests that rural churches, for example, would do well with service projects and fellowship opportunities in their congregations and communities. Seminars and fairs on themes of community or church interest would be effective in urban and suburban churches of this study.

Take advantage of areas of weakness by directing special ministry toward them. Selective preaching and teaching can be done. Testimonies can be given to motivate others in the effective practice of spiritual disciplines. Newsletter topics and church website information can also contain teaching in needed areas. Rural churches might encourage men's/women's retreats to teach silence and study. Suburban churches would benefit from church-wide education on fasting as it is exemplified in Scripture.

CONSIDER THE DIFFERENCES

Certainly there are differences in correlations among the urban, suburban and rural settings. They provide food for thought and questions to consider.

Silence and integrity show totally opposite correlations between suburban and rural settings. The most obvious factor in this difference seems to be environment. The correlation is very strong in the urban church as well. In both the urban and suburban settings these groups are looking for peace. They may work in jobs that are full of noise and stress, and they may long for silence. In the rural setting, silence is much more prevalent than in the urban and suburban settings but perhaps not as valued for spiritual reasons.

The very strong correlations reflected in the suburban setting made sense, but the negative correlations in urban and rural settings are more difficult to understand. The rural setting views life very pragmatically. There is indifference in the rural setting about study in that it is not valued as highly as in urban and suburban settings. This may explain the low correlation in rural settings, but not in the urban setting. Could it be that suburban pastors are more highly educated than their urban and rural counterparts? Does the suburban setting provide a much higher affluence level than in the rural and urban settings?

If so, do urban churches have the money to hire more leaders to share the workload so that each has more time to develop CSDs in his or her life?

There is a very strong correlation of study and hope in suburban settings. This was not seen in all three settings. Where does hope come from in the urban and rural settings? One would think that hope would be required more in an urban setting, but the correlation does not reflect this idea. Hope seems to be something that people in all environments are looking for. Why is it so valued in the suburban setting? How is it possible that there could be a very strong correlation, almost a direct relationship, in suburban and rural settings with regard to study and hope, and a negative correlation in urban? What could be so different for leaders in these different settings with regard to study and hope? The suburban setting is full of hopeful people. People are looking to move away from something bad or moving toward something good. In the urban setting, hope may be a bit thin. As for the rural community, pragmatism may win over hope.

The correlation of service and faith is very strong in the rural setting and very low in the urban setting. The spiritual discipline of service receives a very strong correlation in both the suburban and rural settings but not in the urban. The same idea can be seen in the correlations of faith, hope and love connected with service in the urban setting. The exact opposite is true in the rural setting with love and service being low and faith and hope being very strong. In almost every way, the urban setting is an opposite image of the rural setting.

The negative correlation between silence and

integrity in the rural setting becomes the complete opposite in the urban and suburban settings. This data reflects how these settings view removing oneself from others to hear from God and how their beliefs determine their behaviors.

The urban setting links fasting and faith together as reflected by the very strong correlation; but in the suburban setting, the exact opposite can be seen. The most thought–provoking question is why the urban setting correlations are so different from the suburban and rural.

If this study would be done again with more churches or younger leaders or ten years from now, what would the data show? Would it be a worthy pursuit? Or is it enough to know that we should practice spiritual disciplines simply because it pleases God?

chapter eight

Closing Thoughts

Transformed Leadership is absolutely necessary. Leaders dream the dreams and are the ones who are the visionaries in life. They are out front leading and continually keeping others connected with right perspectives. Leaders have a clear view of the main thing. They have the capacity to rally men and women to a common purpose. Leaders have the character to bring confidence and inspiration to others.

God's ideal for a leader is a shepherd. Charles Jefferson shared, "Shepherding work is the work for which humanity is crying."[1] God called the shepherd Moses from the far side of the desert to lead His people. He called the shepherd David from the hills of Bethlehem to rule His people, and He sent the Great Shepherd of the sheep to seek and save that which was lost.

Today's pastor shepherd must now plan the work of transformed leadership for himself, his leaders and his church. The Christian leader is constantly challenged to present a life of spiritual stability, integrity and direction in the course of public ministry.

In his book, *Outliers*, Malcolm Gladwell researches very successful people who go beyond the norm of a particular group.[2] These outliers, as he calls them, have a tendency to affect individuals and groups in very unique ways. They are hard workers who do their best when opportunity presents itself. In the same way but with a higher purpose, leaders who tap into spiritual disciplines have the capacity to move beyond other leaders of similar background and training. Men and women who practice CSDs stand out as effective leaders.

This was a recurring theme of conversation between my first pastor and me. Dean Wisehart taught me that the development of strong leadership in the church rested in the private spiritual disciplines of the leaders. He used these words often, "Model the disciplines and train the leaders." His life was truly a model of disciplines in leadership. This is a lasting legacy worth striving for!

Such a life shows not only the ELMs of enthusiasm, faith, hope, humility, integrity, knowledge, love and vision. Credibility, discernment, confidence in God, wisdom and the fruits of the Spirit are other qualities and more that grace a disciplined life.

Leadership problems arise from the lack of spiritual disciplines in a leader's life. Leading in the wrong direction is a serious problem, but spiritual disciplines help leaders stay connected with God. A leader's confidence is stunted by the lack. When a leader does not seek the Lord, he or she is unprepared to lead biblically and rests on his own abilities and strengths. Hasty decisions are made because leaders do not take the time necessary to seek the face of God. Where there is neglect of CSDs, there is a lack of passion. This often times expresses itself in a leader's poor work ethic, a desire to spurn the needs of people or an entitlement philosophy that takes advantage of the church and may lead to moral failure. If the leader's ambition is to prove or validate himself, the result will be disorder and chaos in the church (Jas. 3).

When struggling leaders create these kinds of problems, the result is that people do not respond to their leadership. Instead of helping draw people to Christ, leaders actually drive them away when they do not practice holiness. The church will be lacking in the plan, power and peace of God when leaders are not spiritual people. When leaders lack spiritual passion, the church is usually lacking as well.

When leaders practice and teach CSDs, the church will benefit. Doing so immediately shifts the responsibility of spiritual growth from the leadership to the individual. The Body of Christ will begin to pray, experience the power of God more evidently, and lives will be changed. The motivation of the leader in any spiritual practice is a huge factor in determining the outcome.

Leaders of a church should intentionally teach the CSDs when they occur in any text or subject being studied. Plan a strategy that incorporates CSDs into the teaching ministry of the church. I have made it a point to teach on CSDs in a series of sermons to show the primacy of the need in individual lives. I conducted Saturday morning seminars on the CSDs for those who desired to attend. In the church I currently pastor, every attendee was encouraged to complete a Personal Development Plan (PDP) that includes CSDs and more (see APPENDIX B).

By all means make sure study, worship and prayer are the focus of every service of the church. Service should be paramount in our identity as the Body of Christ. Confession should be a primary focus in the communion service. During typical church gatherings, CSDs can be emphasized through testimony services. Consider the media opportunities of newsletter, Facebook and church websites to communicate information on CSDs.

The need of the church today is holiness. Spiritual disciplines incorporated into the lives of leaders and pastors will meet this need. Teaching these disciplines is imperative. Practicing these disciplines is vital.

Knute Larson, who mentored me during early years of pastoral work, was correct in saying, "We should never expect what we do not inspect." I have seen the need for this book, raised the questions, reviewed the literature, conducted the study, received the data, consulted the Scripture, compiled the correlations and drawn the conclusions. Now, may transformed leadership begin with you.

APPENDIX A – LEADERS' QUESTIONNAIRE

☞ Please identify yourself by circling the appropriate description:

21-40 yrs.   41-60 yrs.   61-80 yrs.   81-100 yrs.

Elder   Deacon   Pastor

Male   Female

☞ Please answer the questions quickly without laboring over each one. Your first response is the one I am interested in. Read the question, and then circle the response that best answers the question.

1 = Never

2 = Seldom

3 = Average

4 = Often

5 = Always

143

You have the ability to perceive where God is working and can motivate members of the congregation to move in that direction.	1	2	3	4	5
Strong excitement of feeling describes you.	1	2	3	4	5
You set aside time each day for prayer.	1	2	3	4	5
You respond pridefully when confronted with sin or corrective instruction.	1	2	3	4	5
You have a firm moral code and live by it.	1	2	3	4	5
You remember God throughout your day.	1	2	3	4	5
You have a regular time in the scripture and you only live life according to biblical principles.	1	2	3	4	5
You regularly invite God to search your heart.	1	2	3	4	5
People are agents of growth to you.	1	2	3	4	5
You are dependent on God alone.	1	2	3	4	5
You carry out a plan for strategically studying the Bible.	1	2	3	4	5
Serving others allows you to feel His presence.	1	2	3	4	5

Appendix A - Leaders' Questionnaire

You hear God speak through the Word.	1	2	3	4	5
You are a fully devoted follower of Christ.	1	2	3	4	5
You understand God's presence and calling in your life with great clarity.	1	2	3	4	5
You strive to love God with all your heart, mind and soul, and love your neighbor as yourself.	1	2	3	4	5
You are able to see what needs to happen in church life and clearly communicate that to others.	1	2	3	4	5
Passion characterizes all that you do.	1	2	3	4	5
You keep track of answers to prayers.	1	2	3	4	5
You deal personally and quickly with painful repentance and public confession.	1	2	3	4	5
The quality of being complete or undivided characterizes you.	1	2	3	4	5
You sing praise songs during the course of your day.	1	2	3	4	5
You have a learner's heart and mind.	1	2	3	4	5
You are very honest about your sin before God.	1	2	3	4	5

People in your life are seen as a help to you.	1	2	3	4	5
You make it a habit to fast from food.	1	2	3	4	5
You think of ways to put the Bible into practice.	1	2	3	4	5
Your heart is broken by hearing about the needs of others.	1	2	3	4	5
You enjoy going through your day without a television or phone.	1	2	3	4	5
You have sensitivity to God's activity and act upon it.	1	2	3	4	5
You long expectantly for things.	1	2	3	4	5
You genuinely care about others.	1	2	3	4	5
You have unusual discernment and foresight about matters.	1	2	3	4	5
Worthy causes of all kinds are of great interest to you and you find yourself being attached to them.	1	2	3	4	5
When you pray, your troubles become part of the prayer.	1	2	3	4	5
The position you serve in is one provided by God and you desire not to be big-headed about that.	1	2	3	4	5

Appendix A - Leaders' Questionnaire

Honesty describes you absolutely.	1	2	3	4	5
Enjoyment in your life overflows with praise.	1	2	3	4	5
A keen awareness describes you completely.	1	2	3	4	5
You daily confess your sin to God.	1	2	3	4	5
You seek out people who can help your spiritual walk.	1	2	3	4	5
You make it a habit to fast from television.	1	2	3	4	5
You study the Bible by focusing on one book at a time.	1	2	3	4	5
You find intimacy with God when serving others.	1	2	3	4	5
You need stimulation from phone, television, or radio during your day.	1	2	3	4	5
Belief and trust describe you well.	1	2	3	4	5
You desire for and expect things.	1	2	3	4	5
You have a heart to seek people out and respond to them.	1	2	3	4	5
You communicate ideas in a way that captures the imagination of people.	1	2	3	4	5

Giving yourself completely to whatever engages your interest characterizes your life.	1	2	3	4	5
You keep a current list of prayer requests.	1	2	3	4	5
You accept the rebuke of another easily.	1	2	3	4	5
Taking the "high road" on the issues of life is the only way for you to live.	1	2	3	4	5
You see God as He is: high and lifted up.	1	2	3	4	5
You search for truths and facts above all else.	1	2	3	4	5
As soon as you commit a sin, you confess your sin to God.	1	2	3	4	5
Serving others is a primary motive in your life.	1	2	3	4	5
You make it a habit to fast from the phone.	1	2	3	4	5
You study scripture daily.	1	2	3	4	5
You are able to discern needs when in conversations with others.	1	2	3	4	5
Periods of silence are confusing and uncomfortable to you.	1	2	3	4	5
You have a firm adherence to promises.	1	2	3	4	5

You have a firm belief in fulfillment.	1	2	3	4	5
You have enthusiasm and devotion toward God.	1	2	3	4	5
Provoking, imagining and reminding describe you.	1	2	3	4	5
People think of you as inspiring.	1	2	3	4	5
You pray passages of Scripture for people.	1	2	3	4	5
A willingness to listen to others and respond to their counsel is your desire.	1	2	3	4	5
Let your yes be yes and your no be no characterizes the way you live.	1	2	3	4	5
You find ways to enjoy God during your day.	1	2	3	4	5
You exhibit knowledge and intelligence to a high degree on most things.	1	2	3	4	5
You find it easy to ask God to forgive you.	1	2	3	4	5
You love others with no strings attached.	1	2	3	4	5
You make it a habit to fast from spending money.	1	2	3	4	5
When you hear or read the Bible, you write down thoughts.	1	2	3	4	5

You serve by helping others in need.	1	2	3	4	5
You love to be alone.	1	2	3	4	5
You have a firm adherence to observing duty.	1	2	3	4	5
You have reliance in promises made.	1	2	3	4	5
You have brotherly/sisterly concern for others.	1	2	3	4	5

APPENDIX B – PERSONAL DEVELOPMENT PLAN

Prayerfully consider the following suggestions for spiritual growth and check the ones that the Holy Spirit is leading you to work on this year.

I will commit to go HIGH: (worship)

★ By being baptized …when _____

★ By increasing my worship service attendance

_____

★ By increasing my participation in the worship services (singing, clapping, etc.)_____

_____

★ By increasing my giving to the Lord _____

_____

★ By increasing my daily personal worship time (amount of time or # of days)_____

_____

★ By joining the praise team (musicians, singers, sound/video techs, drama)_____

_____

★ Other _____

I will commit to go DEEP: (fellowship & discipleship)

★ By increasing my prayer life in these ways ____

_____

★ By committing to read through the Bible in one year

★ By memorizing _____ Scripture verses/week

★ By increasing my reading of good Christian literature (authors like Chuck Swindoll, Francis Chan, Max Lucado, John MacArthur, John Maxwell, John Piper, Philip Yancey)

★ By joining the church as a member

★ By joining a Life Group

★ By attending Adult Bible Fellowship (ABF) or Sunday school

★ By attending the Leadership seminar with Pastor

- ★ By attending Men's Ministry activities
- ★ By attending Women's Ministry activities
- ★ By learning about and exercising new spiritual disciplines (prayer, Scripture memory, Bible study, fasting, etc.) _____

_____

- ★ By cutting out ungodly influences in my life

_____

- ★ By meeting with a accountability partner or group
- ★ By giving up bad habits
- ★ By limiting my television intake to _____ hours per day
- ★ Other _____

I will commit to go WIDE: (evangelism and ministry)

- ★ By committing to share Jesus verbally on a regular basis
- ★ By praying for unbelievers on a regular basis

_____

- ★ By calling our church's weekly guests
- ★ By reaching out to my neighbors through serving and spending time with them
- ★ By going on a short-term missions trip this year
- ★ By regularly inviting friends and neighbors to church

★ By giving a testimony in church of how God is working in my life

★ By increasing giving to Calvary Community Church missions offerings

★ By joining a commission team at church (finance team, worship team, property team, Christian Education team, missions team, cleaning team, mowing and grounds team)

★ By serving in a ministry in the community

★ By vising the sick and homebound

★ Other _____

I will commit to go LONG: (discipling the next generation)

★ By increasing time in prayer for my children

★ By starting/improving family devotions at home

★ By teaching the Bible to my children

★ By developing a discipleship plan for my children

★ By starting/improving prayer time with my spouse

★ By making time to date my spouse

★ By teaching or assisting in a children's Sunday school class

★ By serving in children's church time or AWANA Clubs

★ By mentoring a young believer

Appendix B - Personal Development Plan

★ By serving in youth ministry as a sponsor

★ By curbing personal spending and getting out of debt

★ Other _____

End Notes

Chapter One: The Prerequisite

1. Robert Anderson, *Effective Pastor* (Chicago: Moody Press, 1985), 3.

2. Francois Fenelon, *Christian Perfection* (New York: Harper & Row, 1947), 119.

3. Charles Bridges, *Christian Ministry* (Carlisle, PA: Banner of Truth, 1983), 24-25.

4. Fenelon, *Christian Perfection,* 158.

5. Gordon MacDonald, *Rebuilding Your Broken World* (Nashville: Nelson, 1988), 107.

6. Ibid., 50

7. Ibid., 52.

8. Gary Lee Taylor. *Spiritual Disciplines in the Act and Development of Leadership* (Portland, OR: Western Seminary, 2011), 13-14.

9. J. Oswald Sanders, *Spiritual Leadership* (Chicago: Moody Press, 1986), 140-141.

10. M. Robert Mulholland, *Invitation to a Journey* (Downers Grove, IL: InterVarsity, 1993), 104.

11. Ibid., 30.

Chapter Two: The Mandate

1. Fenelon, *Christian Perfection*, 76.

2. Thomas D. Lea and Hayne P. Griffin, Jr. *1-2 Timothy, Titus* (Nashville: Broadman, 1992), 106-114, 278-282.

3. Homer A. Kent Jr., *Pastoral Epistles* (Chicago: Moody Press, 1979), 125-130.

4. Albert Mohler, *Conviction to Lead* (Minneapolis: Bethany House, 2012), 80.

5. Peter H. Davids, *First Epistle of Peter* (Grand Rapids: Eerdmans, 1990), 178-180.

6. E. Glenn Wagner, *Escape from Church, Inc.* (Grand Rapids: Zondervan, 1999), 162.

7. David Dickson, *Elder and His Work* (Phillipsburg, NJ: P & R Publishing, 2004), 26.

8. Rick Gregory, "Shepherding the Congregation," *Voice* 92, no. 1 (January-February 2013): 12.

Chapter Three: The Pastor Shepherd

1. William F. Arndt and F. Wilbur Gingrich, *Greek-English Lexicon of the New Testament and Other Early Christian Literature* (Chicago: University of Chicago, 1967), 418-419.

2. Jim Rosscup, *An Exposition on Prayer* (Chattanooga, TN: AMG, 2011), 4 vols.

3. David Wiersbe, *Dynamics of Pastoral Care* (Grand Rapids: Baker, 2000), 18.

4. Gordon MacDonald, "To Serve and Protect," *Leadership Journal* 33, no. 4 (Fall 2012): 37.

5. Charles Edward Jefferson, *Minister as Shepherd* (New York: Thomas Crowell, 1912), 87.

Chapter Four: Core Spiritual Disciplines

1. M. Robert Mulholland, *Shaped by the Word* (Nashville: Upper Room, 1985), 19.

2. Jefferson, *Minister as Shepherd,* 29.

3. Jerry Bridges, *Discipline of Grace* (Colorado Springs, CO: NavPress, 1994), 46-47.

4. Jan Johnson, *Spiritual Disciplines Companion* (Downers Grove, IL: InterVarsity, 2009), 8. The sixteen spiritual disciplines are: solitude, silence, service, secrecy, prayer, listening, study, meditation, community, submission, reflection, confession, simplicity, fasting, worship and celebration.

5. R. Kent Hughes, *Disciplines of a Godly Man* (Wheaton, IL: Crossway, 2000), 206. The sixteen spiritual disciplines are: purity, marriage, fatherhood, friendship, mind, devotion, prayer, worship, integrity, tongue, work, church, leadership, giving, witness and ministry.

6. Adele Calhoun, *Spiritual Disciplines Handbook* (Downers Grove, IL: InterVarsity, 2005), 11-13. The sixty-two disciplines are: celebration, gratitude, holy communion, rule of life, Sabbath, worship, contemplation, examen, journaling, practice the

presence, rest, retreat, self-care, simplicity, slowing, teachability, unplugging, confession, self-examination, detachment, secrecy, silence, spiritual direction, submission, accountability partner, chastity, community, covenant group, discipling, hospitality, mentoring, service, small group, spiritual friendship, unity, witness, Bible study, devotional reading, meditation, memorization, care of the earth, compassion, control of the tongue, humility, justice, stewardship, truth telling, breath prayer, centering prayer, contemplative prayer, conversational prayer, fasting, fixed-hour prayer, inner-healing prayer, intercessory prayer, labyrinth prayer, liturgical prayer, partners prayer, praying Scripture, prayer recollection and prayer walking.

7. Dallas Willard, *Spirit of Disciplines* (San Francisco: Harper & Row, 1988), 158. The fifteen spiritual disciplines are: solitude, silence, fasting, frugality, chastity, secrecy, sacrifice, study, worship, celebration, service, prayer, fellowship, confession and submission.

8. Ruth Haley Barton, *Sacred Rhythms* (Downers Grove, IL: InterVarsity, 2006), 187. The twenty-two spiritual disciplines are: silence, self-examination, breath prayer, Scripture reflection, solitude, attending to desire, prayer, community, spiritual friendship, discernment, Sabbath, rule of life, confession, examen of consciousness, self-knowledge, celebration, forgiveness, caring for the body, exercise, Scripture, worship in community and listening to the body.

9. Stephen A. Macchia, *Becoming a Healthy Disciple* (Grand Rapids: Baker, 2004), 74-84. The five spir-

itual disciplines are: prayer, Scripture, reflection, proactivity and accountability.

10. Johanes Quasten and Joseph C. Plumpe, eds., *Ancient Christian Writers* (New York: Newman Press, 1978), 6:19.

11. Mulholland, *Invitation to a Journey*, 146.

12. Mark Driscoll and Gerry Breshears, *Doctrine* (Wheaton, IL: Crossway, 2010), 311.

13. Mulholland, *Invitation to a Journey*, 149.

14. Dietrich Bonheoffer, *Life Together* (New York: Harper & Row, 1954), 36.

15. Leon Morris, *Epistle to the Romans* (Grand Rapids: Eerdmans, 1987), 444.

16. John Murray, *Epistle to the Romans* (Grand Rapids: Eerdmans, 1979), 132.

17. Mulholland, *Invitation to a Journey*, 108.

18. Fenelon, *Christian Perfection*, 6.

19. Dallas Willard. *Divine Conspiracy* (San Francisco: HarperCollins, 1998), 235.

20. David Hansen, *Long Wandering Prayer* (Downers Grove, IL: InterVarsity, 2001), 41.

21. Willard, *Spirit of Disciplines*, 182.

22. Ibid., 184.

23. Warren Wiersbe, *On Being a Servant of God* (Nashville: Nelson, 1993), 14.

24. Robert Alden, *Psalms* (Chicago: Moody Press, 1974), 115.

25. Ruth Haley Barton, *Strengthening the Soul of Your*

Leadership (Downers Grove, IL: InterVarsity, 2008), 28.

26. Ruth Haley Barton, *Invitation to Solitude* (Downers Grove, IL: InterVarsity, 2010), 31.

27. Calhoun, *Spiritual Disciplines Handbook,* 164.

28. Johnson, *Spiritual Disciplines Companion,* 127.

29. Ibid., 117.

30. James L. Boyer, *For a World Like Ours* (Winona Lake, IN: BMH, 1971), 40.

31. C. K. Barrett, *First Epistle to the Corinthians* (New York: Harper & Row, 1968), 77.

32. Calhoun, *Spiritual Disciplines Handbook,* 25.

33. Johnson, *Spiritual Disciplines Companion,* 127.

34. Robert E. Webber, *Worship Is a Verb* (Peabody, MA: Hendrickson, 1992), 25.

35. Ibid., 25.

36. Fenelon, *Christian Perfection,* 178.

37. G. K. Beale, *We Become What We Worship* (Downers Grove, IL: InterVarsity, 2008), 216-217.

38. Bryan Chapell, *Christ-Centered Worship* (Grand Rapids: Baker, 2009), 18.

Chapter Five: Effective Leadership Marks

1. Jewel Gingerich Longenecker, "The Path," *Journal of Applied Christian Leadership* 2, no. 2 (Summer 2008): 4.

2. John MacArthur, *Book on Leadership* (Nashville: Nelson, 2004), vi.

End Notes

3. Glenn Daman, *Leading the Small Church* (Grand Rapids: Kregel, 2006), 33.

4. MacArthur, *Book on Leadership,* viii.

5. James M. Kouzes and Barry Z. Posner, *Credibility* (San Francisco: Jossey-Bass, 1993), 185.

6. Craig Perrin, "Remodeling Leaders," *Leadership Excellence* 27, no. 7 (July 2010): 17.

7. Ken Blanchard and Phil Hodges, *Lead Like Jesus* (Nashville: Word, 2005), 4.

8. David Hocking, *Seven Laws of Leadership* (Ventura, CA: Regal, 1991), 22.

9. Robert J. Spitzer, *Spirit of Leadership* (Provo, UT: Executive Excellence, 2000), 257.

10. Hudson T. Amerding, *Spiritual Leadership* (Wheaton, IL: Tyndale, 1978), 115.

11. Ibid., 106.

12. J. Grant Howard, *Spiritual Leadership,* Unpublished Class Notes (Portland, OR.: Western Conservative Baptist Seminary, 1985).

13. Andy Stanley, *Next Generation Leader* (Sisters, OR: Multnomah, 2003), 53.

14. James Stalker, *Life of St. Paul* (Grand Rapids: Zondervan, 1950), 9.

15. C. K. Barrett, *Paul* (Louisville: Westminster/John Knox, 1994), 159.

16. Ibid., 159.

17. Gene A. Getz, *Walk* (Nashville: Broadman & Holman, 1994), 19.

18. Moyer V. Hubbard, *Christianity in the Greco-Roman World* (Grand Rapids: Baker, 2010), 158.

19. Spitzer, *Spirit of Leadership,* 13.

20. James M. Kouzes and Barry Z. Posner. *Leadership Challenge* (San Francisco: Jossey-Bass, 2002), 48.

21. Dallas Willard, *Hearing God* (Downers Grove, IL: InterVarsity, 1999), 156.

22. Barrett, *Paul,* 102.

23. Katharine Doob Sakenfeld, ed., *The New Interpreter's Dictionary of the Bible* (Nashville: Abingdon, 2006), 2:888.

24. Hansen, *Long Wandering Prayer,* 146.

25. Thomas R. Schreiner, *Paul* (Downers Grove, IL: InterVarsity, 2001), 271.

26. Ibid., 272.

27. Alan Andrews, *Kingdom Life* (Colorado Springs, CO: NavPress, 2010), 71.

28. Spitzer, *Spirit of Leadership,* 14.

29. Ibid., 226.

30. Sakenfeld, *The New Interpreter's Dictionary of the Bible,* 3:716.

31. Ibid., 3:717.

32. Frank Northen Magill, *Christian Spirituality* (New York: Harper & Row, 1988), 77.

33. Herman Ridderbos, *Paul* (Grand Rapids:Eerdmans, 1975), 293.

34. David Fisher, *21ˢᵗ Century Pastor* (Grand Rapids: Zondervan, 1996), 161.

35. Bill Hybels, *Axiom* (Grand Rapids: Zondervan, 2008), 30.

36. James M. Kouzes and Barry Z. Posner, *Leader's Legacy* (San Francisco: Jossey-Bass, 2006), 99.

Chapter Six: Theological Support

1. Mark Driscoll and Gerry Breshears, *Vintage Church* (Wheaton, IL.: Crossway, 2008), 25-61.

2. Donald S. Whitney, *Spiritual Disciplines for the Christian Life* (Colorado Springs, CO: NavPress, 1991), 14.

3. Thomas R. Schreiner, *New Testament Theology* (Grand Rapids: Baker, 2008), 375-376.

4. Richard L. Holland, "The Pastor's Sanctifying Role in the Church," *Master's Seminary Journal* 21, no. 2 (Fall 2010): 218.

5. Ibid., 216.

6. Andrew Murray, *Holiest of All* (New Kensington, PA: Whitaker, 2004), 176.

Chapter Seven: Eyes on the Prize

1. Stuart Berg Flexner, ed., *Random House Unabridged Dictionary* (New York: Random House, 1993), 455.

2. Frederick Gravetter and Larry Wallnau, *Essential of Statistics for the Behavioral Sciences* (Pacific Grove, CA: Wadsworth, 2002), 388.

3. The similarities between prayer and worship data correlations are identical and are verified in the original statistical data.

Chapter Eight: Plan the Work

1. Jefferson, *Minister as Shepherd*, 104 .

2. Malcolm Gladwell, *Outliers* (New York: Little, Brown and Company, 2008), 17.

Bibliography

Alden, Robert. *Psalms.* Chicago: Moody Press, 1974.

Alexander, Archibald. *Thoughts on Religious Experience.* Philadelphia: Presbyterian Board of Publication, 1844.

Amerding, Hudson T. *Spiritual Leadership.* Wheaton, IL: Tyndale, 1978.

Anderson, Robert. *Effective Pastor.* Chicago: Moody Press, 1985.

Andrews, Alan. *Kingdom Life.* Colorado Springs, CO: NavPress, 2010.

Arndt, William F. and F. Wilbur Gingrich. *Greek-English Lexicon of the New Testament and Other Early Christian Literature.* Chicago: University of Chicago, 1967.

Barrett, C. K. *First Epistle to the Corinthians.* New York: Harper & Row, 1968.

_____. *Paul.* Louisville: Westminster/John Knox, 1994.

Barton, Ruth Haley. *Invitation to Solitude and Silence.* Downers Grove, IL: InterVarsity, 2010.

_____. *Sacred Rhythms.* Downers Grove, IL.: InterVarsity, 2006.

_____. *Strengthening the Soul of Your Leadership.* Downers Grove, IL: InterVarsity, 2008.

Beale, G. K. *We Become What We Worship.* Downers Grove, IL: InterVarsity, 2008.

Blanchard, Ken and Phil Hodges. *Lead Like Jesus.* Nashville: Word, 2005.

Bonheoffer, Dietrich. *Life Together.* New York: Harper & Row, 1954.

Boston, Thomas. *Human Nature in its Fourfold State.* Philadelphia: Towar and J. and D.M. Hogan, 1830.

Boyer, James L. *For a World Like Ours.* Winona Lake, IN: BMH, 1971.

Bridges, Charles. *Christian Ministry.* Carlisle, PA: Banner of Truth, 1983.

Bridges, Jerry. *Discipline of Grace.* Colorado Springs, CO: NavPress, 1994.

Calhoun, Adele. *Spiritual Disciplines Handbook.* Downers Grove, IL: InterVarsity, 2005.

Chapell, Bryan. *Christ-Centered Worship.* Grand Rapids: Baker, 2009.

Daman, Glenn. *Leading the Small Church.* Grand Rapids: Kregel, 2006.

Davids, Peter H. *First Epistle of Peter.* Grand Rapids: Eerdmans, 1990.

Dickson, David. *Elder and His Work.* Phillipsburg, NJ: P & R Publishing, 2004.

Bibliography

Driscoll, Mark and Gerry Breshears. *Doctrine.* Wheaton, IL: Crossway, 2010.

_____. *Vintage Church.* Wheaton, IL: Crossway, 2008.

Fenelon, Francois. *Christian Perfection.* New York: Harper & Row, 1947.

Fisher, David. *21ˢᵗ Century Pastor.* Grand Rapids: Zondervan, 1996.

Flexner, Stuart Berg, ed. *Random House Unabridged Dictionary.* New York: Random House, 1993.

Getz, Gene A. *Walk.* Nashville: Broadman & Holman, 1994.

Gladwell, Malcolm. *Outliers.* New York: Little, Brown and Company, 2008.

Gravetter, Frederick and Larry Wallnau. *Essentials of Statistics for the Behavioral Sciences.* Pacific Grove, CA: Wadsworth, 2002.

Gregory, Rick. "Shepherding the Congregation," *Voice* 92, no. 1 (January-February 2013): 12-14.

Hansen, David. *Long Wandering Prayer.* Downers Grove, IL: InterVarsity, 2001.

Henrichsen, Walter A. *Disciples Are Made – Not Born.* Wheaton, IL: Victor, 1974.

Henry, Matthew. *Communicant's Companion.* New York: L. and F. Lockwood, 1819.

Hocking, David. *Seven Laws of Leadership.* Ventura, CA: Regal, 1991.

Holland, Richard L. "The Pastor's Sanctifying Role in the Church," *The Master's Seminary Journal* 21, no. 2 (Fall 2010): 215-229.

Holy Bible: New International Version. Grand Rapids: Zondervan, 1983.

Howard, J. Grant. *Spiritual Leadership.* Unpublished Class Notes. Portland, OR: Western Conservative Baptist Seminary, 1985.

Hubbard, Moyer V. *Christianity in the Greco-Roman World.* Grand Rapids: Baker, 2010.

Hughes, R. Kent. *Disciplines of a Godly Man.* Wheaton, IL: Crossway, 2000.

Hunter, James C. *Servant.* New York: Crown Business, 1998.

Hybels, Bill. *Axiom.* Grand Rapids: Zondervan, 2008.

_____. *Courageous Leadership.* Grand Rapids: Zondervan, 2002.

Jefferson, Charles Edward. *Minister as Shepherd.* New York: Thomas Crowell, 1912.

Johnson, Jan. *Spiritual Disciplines Companion.* Downers Grove, IL: InterVarsity, 2009.

Kent, Homer A, Jr. *Pastoral Epistles.* Chicago: Moody Press, 1979.

Kouzes, James M. and Barry Z. Posner. *Credibility.* San Francisco: Jossey-Bass, 1993.

_____. *Leader's Legacy.* San Francisco: Jossey-Bass, 2006.

_____. *Leadership Challenge.* San Francisco: Jossey-Bass, 2002.

Lea, Thomas D. and Hayne P. Griffin, Jr. *1-2 Timothy, Titus.* Nashville: Broadman, 1992.

Longenecker, Jewel Gingerich. "The Path," *Journal*

Bibliography

of Applied Christian Leadership 2, no. 2 (Summer 2008): 4-5.

MacArthur, John. *Book on Leadership.* Nashville: Nelson, 2004.

Macchia, Stephen A. *Becoming a Healthy Disciple.* Grand Rapids: Baker, 2004.

MacDonald, Gordon. *Rebuilding Your Broken World.* Nashville: Nelson, 1988.

_____. "To Serve and Protect" *Leadership Journal* 33, no. 4 (Fall 2012): 35-38.

Magill, Frank Northen. *Christian Spirituality.* New York: Harper & Row, 1988.

Mohler, Albert. *Conviction to Lead.* Minneapolis: Bethany House, 2012.

Morris, Leon. *Epistle to the Romans.* Grand Rapids: Eerdmans, 1987.

Mulholland, M. Robert. *Invitation to a Journey.* Downers Grove, IL: InterVarsity, 1993.

_____. *Shaped by the Word.* Nashville: Upper Room, 1985.

Murray, Andrew. *Holiest of All.* New Kensington, PA: Whitaker, 2004.

Murray, John. *Epistle to the Romans.* Grand Rapids: Eerdmans, 1979.

Perrin, Craig. "Remodeling Leaders" *Leadership Excellence* 27, no. 7 (July 2010): 17.

Quastan, Johanes and Joseph C. Plumpe, eds. *Ancient Christian Writers.* 10 vols. New York: Newman Press, 1978.

Ridderbos, Herman. *Paul.* Grand Rapids: Eerdmans, 1975.

Rosscup, Jim. *An Exposition On Prayer.* 4 vols. Chattanooga, TN: AMG, 2011.

Sakenfeld, Katharine Doob, ed. *New Interpreter's Dictionary of the Bible.* 5 vols. Nashville: Abingdon Press, 2006.

Sanders, J. Oswald. *Spiritual Leadership.* Chicago: Moody Press, 1986.

Schreiner, Thomas R. *New Testament Theology.* Grand Rapids: Baker, 2008.

_____. *Paul.* Downers Grove, IL: InterVarsity, 2001.

Smith, John. *Lectures on the Nature and End of the Sacred Office.* Baltimore: A. Neal, 1810.

Spitzer, Robert J. *Spirit of Leadership.* Provo, UT: Executive Excellence, 2000.

Stalker, James. *Life of St. Paul.* Grand Rapids: Zondervan, 1950.

Stanley, Andy. *Next Generation Leader.* Sisters, OR: Multnomah, 2003.

Taylor, Gary Lee. *Role of Spiritual Disciplines in the Development and Act of Leadership.* Dissertation (D. Min.). Portland, OR: Western Seminary, 2011.

Taylor, Jeremy. *Rule and Exercises of Holy Living.* London: Bell and Daldy Fleet Street, 1857.

Wagner, E. Glenn. *Escape from Church, Inc.* Grand Rapids: Zondervan, 1999.

Webber, Robert E. *Worship is a Verb.* Peabody, MA: Hendrickson, 1992.

Bibliography

Whitney, Donald S. *Spiritual Disciplines for the Christian Life.* Colorado Springs, CO: NavPress, 1991.

Wiersbe, David. *Dynamics of Pastoral Care.* Grand Rapids: Baker, 2000.

Wiersbe, Warren. *On Being a Servant of God.* Nashville: Nelson, 1993.

Willard, Dallas. *Divine Conspiracy.* San Francisco: HarperCollins, 1998.

_____. *Hearing God.* Downers Grove, IL: InterVarsity, 1999.

_____. *Spirit of Disciplines.* San Francisco: Harper & Row, 1988.

CPSIA information can be obtained at www.ICGtesting.com
Printed in the USA
BVOW071909110313

315251BV00001B/1/P